TABLE OF CONTENTS

I0423397

Page

TABLE OF CONTENTS (Continued)

Page

INTRODUCTION

This Directory has been prepared as a guidebook to locate and identify organizations and individuals at the state and national level who have a responsibility to disclose information on money in politics.

The term "money in politics" has been given a broad definition to include federal and state campaign finance reports, lobby reports, personal financial statements, public financing, state initiative/referendum spending, and a wide range of other financial filings.

The offices listed are those which have the primary responsibility to disclose the information. These include federal agencies, Secretaries of State, state commissions, boards and election offices. In some states, one office handles all the disclosure whereas in others, as many as four different offices handle disclosure. There may also be an additional office, such as the Office of the Attorney General, which has responsibility for issuing advisory opinions or enforcement actions. This type of office has been included since it may be involved in other court actions.

The individuals identified are those who supervise or control the records offices. In addition, other names have been listed when the Federal Election Commission staff has had regular contact with them and/or the state office has wished to list them. These persons may be involved with identification of candidates for the ballot, election results, voting accessibility, informational seminars or other communications. Not all staff members have been listed, but an attempt has been made to include those knowledgeable in the targeted subject areas.

The address and phone number of each office has been listed so that one may quickly contact the proper office. Uniform Resource Locators (URLs) have been included for those offices that maintain a site accessible through the Internet. E-mail addresses for informational requests (rather than for the submission of filings) are listed for those offices that have chosen to include them.

It is hoped the Directory will facilitate communication among disclosure officials across the country. While they work in various offices, they share common concerns: records storage and retrieval; computerization and utilization of other new disclosure technologies; guidance to regulated candidates and committees; assistance to the media and the general public; education of the electorate on the role of money in politics; and, recruitment of public-oriented staff.

EXPLANATION OF DATA

Because there are many different types of reports required by the states, the Directory has been limited to those reports which relate to public officials in the public trust. The Directory is not meant to be a definitive listing of all documents relating to public officials. Instead, it concentrates on reports concerning the use of money in politics, and provides contacts for information on the election process.

When identifying what type of disclosure is available at a specific office, the Directory uses several broad categories which are listed below. These categories have been applied to all the states.

Because state law varies widely (in the level of reporting, the frequency of filing, and the content of the reports), the researcher may find that the value of the data disclosed differs from state to state.

Types of Information

Candidates on Ballot

This notation indicates the office which maintains a list of those who have filed for office and those officially on the ballot. In some cases, persons may have taken earlier steps which indicate candidacy (such as filing a statement of candidacy or campaign finance report, or making a public announcement).

Campaign Finance Reports

State: This category includes reports filed by a variety of candidates or officeholders, political parties, political action committees, special interest committees, political committees, contributors, unions, corporations, and other filers.

Federal: This category includes reports filed by a variety of candidates or officeholders, political parties, political action committees, special interest committees, political committees, contributors, unions, corporations, and other filers. Where "online" is specified, the office is a participant in the Commission's State Filing Waiver Program and provides for public review and printing of federal reports through online electronic access to the Federal Election Commission. Otherwise, disclosure is provided by duplicate paper filings submitted to the state.

Corporate Registration

This category includes registrations and/or reports from public, domestic, foreign or non-profit corporations, charitable organizations, or professional fundraisers.

Election Results

This notation indicates the office which maintains the vote results on a statewide basis. Because elections are controlled at the local, municipal or county level in many states, the results may not reach this office immediately after the election.

Electronic Filings

This notation indicates that the office currently receives, and makes available on the Internet, filings submitted electronically. The method of transmission to the office may be via computer disk, a direct modem connection or the Internet.

Lobbying

This category includes reports from lobbyists, employers of lobbyists, clients, or contributions of lobbyists to campaigns.

Other Court Actions

This notation indicates other state officials who may handle or assist in prosecutorial actions or constitutional challenges of state laws. In some states, agencies may divide or share certain authority in the areas of hearings, fines, subpoena of witnesses, civil penalties, criminal penalties, etc.

Personal Finance Reports

State: This category includes Ethics Act filings, conflict of interest reports, personal wealth statements, outside employment and outside income reports, and statements of substantial interest.

Federal: The office listed receives, from the Secretary of the U.S. Senate and the Clerk of the U.S. House of Representatives, reports filed by Members and candidates under Title I of the Ethics in Government Act of 1978.

Public Financing

This category includes only reports which are available to the public. These generally involve matching fund requests or reports on disbursement of public fund grants.

Spending on Initiatives/Referendums

This category includes reports from entities spending and/or collecting funds for ballot questions, public questions, ballot issues, initiatives, referendums, and propositions.

Voting Accessibility

This notation indicates the state level office which handles implementation of portions of the Voting Accessibility for the Elderly and Handicapped Act (PL-98-435). This primarily relates to the accessibility of polling places.

Corrections, Deletions, Additions

Anyone with information that would improve the Directory should contact Eileen J. Leamon, Deputy Assistant Staff Director for Disclosure, Federal Election Commission, Washington, D.C. 20463. 202/694-1120 or 800/424-9530, option 2 (toll free), 202/501-0693 (FAX), eleamon@fec.gov (e-mail).

FEDERAL ELECTION COMMISSION

999 E Street, N.W.
Washington, D.C. 20463
800/424-9530
202/694-1100
http://www.fec.gov

COMMISSIONERS

Matthew S. Petersen, Chairman

Steven T. Walther, Vice Chairman

Lee E. Goodman, Commissioner

Caroline C. Hunter, Commissioner

Ann M. Ravel, Commissioner

Ellen L. Weintraub, Commissioner

STAFF DIRECTOR – Alec Palmer

ACTING GENERAL COUNSEL – Daniel A. Petalas

INSPECTOR GENERAL – Lynne A. McFarland

ACTING CHIEF FINANCIAL OFFICER – Judy Berning

FEDERAL ELECTION COMMISSION PUBLIC CONTACTS

All of these contacts may be reached by calling the Commission on the toll free line, 800/424-9530.

PUBLIC DISCLOSURE AND MEDIA RELATIONS DIVISION

Judith Ingram, Press Officer and Assistant Staff Director

PUBLIC RECORDS
202/694-1120

Eileen Leamon, Deputy Assistant Staff Director for Disclosure
Jason Bucelato, Senior Public Affairs Specialist
Olivia Farrow, Public Information Specialist
Julie Kinzer, Public Information Specialist
Matthew Rowley, Public Information Specialist

PRESS OFFICE
202/694-1220

Christian Hilland, Deputy Press Officer
Julia Queen, Public Affairs Specialist
Carmen Gray, Administrative Assistant

INFORMATION DIVISION
202/694-1100

Greg Scott, Assistant Staff Director
Liz Kurland, Deputy Assistant Staff Director for Outreach
George Smaragdis, Deputy Assistant Staff Director for Publications
Dorothy Yeager, Senior Communications Specialist
(Vacant), Senior Communications Specialist
Isaac Baker, Communications Specialist
Chris Berg, Communications Specialist
Kathy Carothers, Communications Specialist
Jonella Culmer, Communications Specialist
Lauren Lambert, Communications Specialist
Myles Martin, Communications Specialist
Zainab Smith, Communications Specialist

LIBRARY
202/694-1600

Leta Holley, Director
Lucia Martinez, Information Specialist

FEDERAL DISCLOSURE OFFICES

FEDERAL DISCLOSURE OFFICES

FEDERAL ELECTION COMMISSION

Public Records Office
999 E Street, N.W., 1st Floor
Washington, D.C. 20463
URL http://www.fec.gov (FEC Home Page)
E-Mail: pubrec@fec.gov
202/694-1120   FAX 202/501-0693
1-800/424-9530, Press 2 (Toll Free)
202/501-3413 (Automated FAX Service)

    Eileen Leamon
    Jason Bucelato
    Olivia Farrow
    Julie Kinzer
    Matthew Rowley

*
*
*
*
*
*
*
*
*
*
*
*
*
*
*
*
*
*
*

-Federal Campaign Finance Reports
-Personal Financial Reports of Presidential
    Candidates (Excluding Incumbent) and
    FEC Commissioners
-Presidential Matching Fund Submissions
-Completed Compliance Cases and Audits
-Completed Litigation Files
-Advisory Opinion Requests and Advisory
    Opinions Issued
-Public Computer Access to FEC Database
-Internet Access to Federal Campaign Finance
    Reports, Summary Figures, Contributor
    Listings, Enforcement Query System and
    Advisory Opinion Search System
-Electronic Filings

OFFICE OF THE SECRETARY OF THE SENATE

Office of Public Records
U.S. Senate
232 Hart Senate Office Building
Washington, D.C. 20510
URL http://www.disclosure.senate.gov
202/224-0322   FAX 202/224-1851

    Dana McCallum, Superintendent
    Erica Omorogieva, Assistant Superintendent
    Samiah Mostafa, Staff Assistant
    Antionette Thompson, Senior Information Specialist
    Malaika Nji, Information Specialist

*
*
*
*
*
*
*
*
*
*
*
*
*
*
*

-Federal Campaign Finance Reports
    (U.S. Senate Only)
-Personal Financial Reports of Senate Members,
    Candidates, Senior Staff, and Legislative
    Agency
-Federal Lobby Reports
-Senate Committee Foreign Travel Reports
-Registration of Mass Mailings
-Reports of Outside Employees Working for Senate
-Revised Gift Rule Filings (Including Travel Paid
    by Non-Governmental Organizations)
-Legal Expense Funds Disclosures

OFFICE OF THE CLERK OF THE HOUSE

Legislative Resource Center
U.S. House of Representatives
135 Cannon House Office Building
Washington, D.C. 20515-6612
URL http://clerk.house.gov
E-Mail: info.clerkweb@mail.house.gov
202/226-5200   FAX 202/226-4874

    R. Dale Thomas, Chief
    Corliss Clemonts-James, Deputy Chief
    Steve Pingeton, Manager, Records and Registration
    Karen Granger, Manager, Public Information
    Rae Ellen Best, House Librarian

*
*
*
*
*
*
*
*
*
*
*
*
*
*
*

-Federal Campaign Finance Reports
-Personal Financial Reports of House Members,
    Candidates and Senior Staff
-Federal Lobby Reports
-Legislative Service Organization Reports
-House Committee Foreign Travel Reports
-Published Reports of Salaries and Expenses
-Revised Gift Rule Filings (Including Travel Paid
    by Non-Governmental Organizations)
-Legal Expense Funds Disclosures

DEPARTMENT OF COMMERCE

Public Information Office
PIO, 8H060
U.S. Census Bureau
Department of Commerce
4600 Silver Hill Road
Suitland, Maryland 20746
General Public: Customer Services Center
301/763-4636 FAX 301/457-3670
1-800/923-8282 (Toll Free)
URL http://www.census.gov and *http://fastfacts.census.gov*
E-Mail: pio@census.gov
    Mailing Address:
    PIO, 8H060
    U.S. Census Bureau
    4600 Silver Hill Road
    Washington, DC 20233

Media: Public Information Office
301/763-3030
URL http://www.census.gov/newsroom
E-Mail: pio@census.gov

-Economic and Demographic Data of U.S. States, Counties and Congressional Districts

DEPARTMENT OF DEFENSE

Matt Boehmer, Director
Federal Voting Assistance Program (FVAP)
Department of Defense
4800 Mark Center Drive, Suite 03J25-02
Alexandria, Virginia 22350-5000
URL http://www.fvap.gov
E-Mail: vote@fvap.gov
571/372-0727 FAX 571/372-0735
1-800/438-8683 (Toll Free)

-Uniformed and Overseas Citizens Absentee Voting Act (UOCAVA)

DEPARTMENT OF HOMELAND SECURITY

Office of Government and Public Affairs
U.S. Secret Service
Department of Homeland Security
245 Murray Drive, Building 410
Washington, D.C. 20223
URL http://www.secretservice.gov
202/406-5708 FAX 202/406-9069

-Secret Service Protection for Presidential Candidates

DEPARTMENT OF JUSTICE

Loretta Lynch
Attorney General of the United States
U.S. Department of Justice
950 Pennsylvania Avenue, N.W.
Washington, D.C. 20530-0001
URL http://www.justice.gov
E-Mail: AskDOJ@usdoj.gov
202/514-2000, 202/353-1555   FAX 202/514-4371

Vanita Gupta, Principal Deputy Assistant Attorney General
Civil Rights Division
202/514-4609   FAX 202/514-0293
TDD 202/514-0716

    Chris Herren, Chief
    Voting Section, Civil Rights Division
    Room 7254-NWB
    U.S. Department of Justice
    950 Pennsylvania Avenue, N.W.
    Washington, D.C. 20530
    URL https://www.justice.gov/crt/voting-section
    E-Mail: voting.section@usdoj.gov
    202/307-2767   FAX 202/307-3961
    1-800/253-3931 (Toll Free)

-Enforcement of Federal civil rights voting laws prohibiting, among other things, discrimination on account of race, color, or membership in a language minority group, and laws protecting voting rights of citizens who are overseas, elderly, illiterate, or handicapped.

Leslie R. Caldwell, Assistant Attorney General
Criminal Division
E-Mail: Criminal.Division@usdoj.gov
202/514-2601   FAX 202/514-9412

    Raymond Hulser, Chief
    Public Integrity Section, Criminal Division
    URL https://www.justice.gov/criminal/pin
    202/514-1412   FAX 202/514-3003

    Richard C. Pilger, Director
    Election Crimes Branch, Criminal Division
    202/514-1421   FAX 202/514-3003

-Enforcement of Federal criminal laws relating to voter fraud, illegal campaign contribution schemes, criminal fraud on federal public campaign financing programs, and criminal patronage abuses. Publishes a volume of federal prosecution of election crimes.

John P. Carlin, Assistant Attorney General
National Security Division
E-Mail: nsd.public@usdoj.gov
202/514-2007 and 202/514-1153   FAX 202/514-5331

    Heather H. Hunt, Chief
    FARA (Foreign Agents Registration Act) Registration Unit
    Department of Justice/NSD
    600 E Street, N.W.
    BICN – Room 1300
    Washington, D.C. 20004
    URL http://www.fara.gov
    E-Mail: fara.public@usdoj.gov
    202/233-0776 and 202-233-0777   FAX 202/233-2147

-Registration of agents representing foreign countries, companies and organizations.

DEPARTMENT OF LABOR

U.S. Department of Labor Office of Labor-Management Standards Public Disclosure Room 200 Constitution Avenue, N.W., Room N-1519 Washington, D.C. 20210 *URL http://www.olms.dol.gov* *E-Mail: olms-public@dol.gov* 202/693-0125 FAX 202/693-1344	-Union Information Reports, Annual Financial Reports, Constitutions and Bylaws

DEPARTMENT OF TREASURY

Office of Legislative and Public Affairs Bureau of the Fiscal Service 401 14th Street, S.W. Washington, D.C. 20227 *URL http://www.fiscal.treasury.gov/fsnews/fs_news.htm* 202/874-6750 and 202/504-3502	-Public Financing System Questions
Information Office Internal Revenue Service *URL http://www.irs.gov* 1-800/829-1040 (Toll Free)	-Tax Check-Off Questions

FEDERAL COMMUNICATIONS COMMISSION

Robert Baker, Assistant Division Chief Office of Political Programming Policy Division, Media Bureau 445 12th Street, S.W. Washington, D.C. 20554 *URL http://www.fcc.gov/mb/policy* *E-Mail: campaignlaw@fcc.gov* 202/418-1440 FAX 202/418-1198	-Inquiries and Complaints Concerning Equal Time, Reasonable Access Relating to Broadcasting, and Publicly Distributed Communications -Electronic Filings
Public Reference Room 445 12th Street, S.W., Room CY-A257 Washington, D.C. 20554 *URL http://www.fcc.gov* 202/418-0270 or 1-888/225-5322 (Toll Free)	

FEDERAL DISCLOSURE OFFICES (Continued)

INTERNAL REVENUE SERVICE

Internal Revenue Service Center
RAIVS Unit, Mail Stop 6716
Ogden, Utah 84201
URL http //www.irs.gov/Charities-&-Non-Profits/Political-Organizations
1-877/829-5500 (Toll Free)   FAX 801/620-7896

(Or, contact the appropriate service center where group is based. Call
1-800/829-1040 for IRS office locations. TDD: 1-800/829-4059.)

Internal Revenue Service
Correspondence Unit
TE/GE Division, Room 4024
P.O. Box 2508
Cincinnati, Ohio 45201
URL https //www.irs.gov/charities-non-profits/political-organizations/eo-customer-account-services
1-877/829-5500 (Toll Free)

-Section 527 Political Organization Filings and
   Exempt Organization Tax Returns (Form 990)

-Tax Exempt and Government Entities Information

NATIONAL ARCHIVES AND RECORDS ADMINISTRATION

Richard H. Hunt, Director
Center for Legislative Archives
700 Pennsylvania Avenue, N.W., Room 8E
Washington, D.C. 20408-0001
URL http://www.archives.gov/legislative
202/357-5350   FAX 202/357-5911

-Federal Campaign Finance Reports Filed Prior to
   1972, under the Federal Corrupt Practices Act.
   [Call prior to visit so documents may be pulled
   from stacks. Fill out researchers form in
   Room 205.]

SECURITIES AND EXCHANGE COMMISSION

Office of FOIA Services
Securities and Exchange Commission
100 F Street, N.E., Room 2465
Washington, D.C. 20549
URL http://www.sec.gov
E-Mail: foiapa@sec.gov
202/551-7900

-Corporate Financial Reports
-Electronic Filings

U.S. ELECTION ASSISTANCE COMMISSION

Brian D. Newby, Executive Director
U.S. Election Assistance Commission
1335 East West Highway, Suite 4300
Silver Spring, Maryland 20910
URL http://www.eac.gov
E-Mail: HAVAinfo@eac.gov
301/563-3919   FAX 301/734-3108
1-866/747-1471 (Toll Free)

   Clifford D. Tatum, General Counsel
   Mohammed Maeruf, Chief Information Officer
   Annette Lafferty, Chief Financial Officer
   Bryan Whitener, Director of Communications and Clearinghouse
   Brian J. Hancock, Director of Voting System Testing and
      Certification
   Karen Lynn-Dyson, Director of Research, Policy & Programs
   Monica Holman Evans, Director of Grants Management

-Help America Vote Act (HAVA)
-National Voter Registration Act (NVRA) and
   National Mail Voter Registration Form
-National Clearinghouse on Election Administration
-Voting Systems Equipment Standards, Testing,
   Certification & Laboratory Accreditation
-Payments and Guidance to States for Election
   Improvements

-11-

FEDERAL DISCLOSURE OFFICES (Continued)

U.S. OFFICE OF GOVERNMENT ETHICS

Walter M. Shaub, Jr., Director
U.S. Office of Government Ethics
1201 New York Avenue, N.W., Suite 500
Washington, D.C. 20005-3917
URL http://www.oge.gov
E-Mail: ContactOGE@oge.gov
202/482-9250   FAX 202/482-9237
TTY 800/877-8339

      David J. Apol, General Counsel
      Shelley Finlayson, Chief of Staff and Program Counsel
      Dale "Chip" Christopher, Deputy Director for Compliance
      Deborah Bortot, Chief for Presidential Nominations

-Executive Financial Disclosure Reports
    (President, Vice President, and Presidential
      Appointees Confirmed by the U.S. Senate)
-Financial Disclosure Reports
(Presidential and Vice President Candidates)

U.S. OFFICE OF SPECIAL COUNSEL

Barbara Wheeler, Chief
Complaints Examining Unit
U.S. Office of Special Counsel
1730 M Street, N.W., Suite 218
Washington, D.C 20036-4505
URL http://www.osc.gov
202/254-3670   FAX 202/653-0015
1-800/872-9855 (Toll Free)

-Investigates and Prosecutes Hatch Act Violations

Hatch Act Unit
202/254-3650   FAX 202/254-3700
1-800/854-2824 (Toll Free)

-Inquiries and Advisory Opinions about the
    Hatch Act

STATE DISCLOSURE OFFICES

SECRETARY OF STATE

John H. Merrill (Elected, R)
Secretary of State
State Capitol, Suite S-105
600 Dexter Avenue
Montgomery, Alabama 36130
URL http://www.sos.alabama.gov
E-Mail: john.merrill@sos.alabama.gov
334/242-7200 FAX 334/242-4993
    Mailing Address:
    P.O. Box 5616
    Montgomery, Alabama 36103-5616

    David A. Z. Brewer, Chief of Staff
    John Bennett, Deputy Chief of Staff

Edward Packard, Elections Director
Elections Division
State Capitol, Suite E-210
600 Dexter Avenue
Montgomery, Alabama 36130
334/242-7210 FAX 334/242-2444
1-800/274-8683 (Toll Free)

- Candidates on Ballot
- Election Results
- Federal Campaign Finance Reports
    (Online via FEC.gov)
- Federal Personal Financial Reports
- State Campaign Finance Reports
- Voting Accessibility
- County Boards of Registrars

Clay Helms, Assistant Elections Director and Supervisor of Voter
    Registration
State Capitol, Suite E-207
600 Dexter Avenue
Montgomery, Alabama 36130
334/353-7177 FAX 334/242-2444
1-800/274-8683 (Toll Free)

- Establishment and Management of a Statewide
    Voter File
- Help America Vote Act (HAVA) Implementation

Joel Laird, General Counsel
State Capitol, Suite E-206
600 Dexter Avenue
Montgomery, Alabama 36130
334/242-0447 FAX 334/353-7344

Elaine Swearingen, Business Entities Director
Alabama State House, Suite 119
11 South Union Street
Montgomery, Alabama 36130
334/353-1931 FAX 334/240-3138

- Corporate Registration

Judy Pickler, UCC Director
Alabama State House, Suite 219
11 South Union Street
Montgomery, Alabama 36130
334/242-7213 FAX 334/240-3138

STATE ETHICS COMMISSION

Thomas B. Albritton, Executive Director
State Ethics Commission
100 North Union Street, Suite 104
Montgomery, Alabama 36104
URL http://www.ethics.alabama.gov
E-Mail: info@ethics.alabama.gov
334/242-2997 FAX 334/242-0248
   Mailing Address:
   P.O. Box 4840
   Montgomery, Alabama 36103-4840

   Hugh R. Evans, III, General Counsel
   334/242-2873

-State Personal Financial Reports
-State Lobby Reports

DEPARTMENT OF REVENUE

Mike Mason, Assistant Commissioner and Disclosure Officer
Department of Revenue
50 North Ripley Street, Room 4112
Montgomery, Alabama 36132
URL http://www.revenue.alabama.gov
E-Mail: mike.mason@revenue.alabama.gov
334/242-1175 FAX 334/242-0550

-Collection of Public Financing Funds

STATE COMPTROLLER

Thomas L. White, Jr., Comptroller
100 North Union Street, Suite 220
Montgomery, Alabama 36130
URL http://comptroller.alabama.gov
E-Mail: tom.white@comptroller.alabama.gov
334/242-7063 FAX 334/242-7466

-Disbursement of Public Financing Funds

LEGISLATIVE REFERENCE

Othni Lathram, Director
Legislative Reference Service
Alabama State House, Suite 613
11 South Union Street
Montgomery, Alabama 36130-3550
URL http://lrs.state.al.us
E-Mail: olathram@ali.state.al.us
334/242-7560 FAX 334/242-4358

ATTORNEY GENERAL

Luther Strange (Elected, R)
Attorney General of Alabama
501 Washington Avenue
Montgomery, Alabama 36130
URL http://www.ago.alabama.gov
334/242-7300 FAX 334/353-9173
    Mailing Address:
    P.O. Box 300152
    Montgomery, Alabama 36130-0152

Brenda Smith, Assistant Attorney General and Chief
Opinions Division
E-Mail: bsmith@ago.state.al.us

*
*   -Other Court Actions
*
*
*
*
*
*
*
*
*
*
*
*

ALASKA

LIEUTENANT GOVERNOR

Byron Mallot (Elected, D)
Lieutenant Governor
State Capitol, Room 315
Juneau, Alaska 99801
URL http://www.ltgov.alaska.gov
907/465-3520   FAX 907/465-5400
  Mailing Address:
  P.O. Box 110015
  Juneau, Alaska 99811-0015

-Federal Campaign Finance Reports
  (Online via FEC.gov)
-Federal Personal Financial Reports

Josie Bahnke, Director
Division of Elections
240 Main Street, Suite 400
Juneau, Alaska 99801
URL http://www.elections.alaska.gov
E-Mail: elections@alaska.gov
907/465-4611   FAX 907/465-3203
TTY 907/465-3020
  Mailing Address:
  P.O. Box 110017
  Juneau, Alaska 99811-0017

  Brian Jackson, Election Program Manager
  Sharon Forrest, Election Coordinator

-Candidates on Ballot
-Election Results
-Voting Accessibility

ALASKA PUBLIC OFFICES COMMISSION

Paul Dauphinais, Executive Director
Alaska Public Offices Commission
2221 East Northern Lights Boulevard, Room 128
Anchorage, Alaska 99508-4149
URL http://doa.alaska.gov/apoc
907/276-4176   FAX 907/276-7018

Heather Dalberg, Paralegal I
Alaska Public Offices Commission - Juneau Office
240 Main Street, Suite 500
Juneau, Alaska 99811-0222
907/465-4864   FAX 907/465-4832
  Mailing Address:
  P.O. Box 110222
  Juneau, Alaska 99811-0222

-State and Municipal Campaign Finance Reports
-State and Municipal Initiative/Referendum
  Spending Reports
-State and Municipal Public Official Financial
  Disclosure Reports
-State Legislative Financial Disclosure Reports
  (Legislators and Legislative Agency Directors)
-State Lobbying Reports
-Electronic Filings

DEPARTMENT OF COMMERCE, COMMUNITY & ECONOMIC DEVELOPMENT

Janey Hovenden, Director
Division of Corporations, Business and Professional Licensing
333 West Willoughby Avenue, 9th Floor
Juneau, Alaska 99801
URL http://www.commerce.state.ak.us
E-Mail: corporations@alaska.gov
907/465-2550   FAX 907/465-2974
TTY 907/465-2297
  Mailing Address:
  P.O. Box 110806
  Juneau, Alaska 99811-0806

-Corporate Registration

SELECT COMMITTEE ON LEGISLATIVE ETHICS

Jerry D. Anderson, Administrator
Select Committee on Legislative Ethics
716 West 4th Street, Suite 217
Anchorage, Alaska 99501
URL http://ethics.legis.state.ak.us
E-Mail: ethics.committee@akleg.gov
907/269-0150 FAX 907/269-0152
    Mailing Address:
    P.O. Box 101468
    Anchorage, Alaska 99510-1468

-Publishes List of Board Memberships, Participation
    in State Benefit and Loan Programs, Close
    Economic Associations, Gifts,
    Representation before State Agencies,
    Interests in State Contracts and Leases
-Enforces Legislative Standards of Conduct
-Issues Advisory Opinions
-Investigates Complaints and Issues Decisions
-Conducts Mandatory Ethics Training for
    Legislators and Legislative Staff

LEGISLATIVE RESEARCH SERVICES

Chuck Burnham, Manager
Legislative Research Services
State Capitol, Room 3
Juneau, Alaska 99801-1182
URL http://akleg.gov/laa/research.php
E-Mail: chuck.burnham@akleg.gov
907/465-3991 FAX 907/465-3908

ATTORNEY GENERAL

Craig W. Richards (Appointed, R)
Attorney General of Alaska
Alaska Department of Law - Office of the Attorney General
P.O. Box 110300
Juneau, Alaska 99811-0300
URL http://www.law.alaska.gov
907/465-3600 FAX 907/465-2075

-Other Court Actions

    Libby Bakalar
    Assistant Attorney General
    Alaska Department of Law - Office of the Attorney General
    P.O. Box 110300
    Juneau, Alaska 99811-0300
    E-Mail: libby.bakalar@alaska.gov
    907/465-3600 FAX 907/465-2075

    Mary Lynn Macsalka
    Assistant Attorney General
    Alaska Department of Law - Office of the Attorney General
    1031 West 4th Avenue
    Anchorage, Alaska 99501
    E-Mail: marylynn.macsalka@alaska.gov
    907/269-5100 FAX 907/258-4978

LIEUTENANT GOVERNOR

Lemanu Peleti Mauga (Elected, D)
Lieutenant Governor
Executive Office Building, 3rd Floor
American Samoa Government
Pago Pago, American Samoa 96799
E-Mail: lt.governor@go.as.gov
684/633-4116   FAX 684/633-2269

ELECTION OFFICE

Uiagalelei Lealofi, Director
American Samoa Election Office
P.O. Box 3970
Pago Pago, American Samoa 96799
URL http://americansamoaelectionoffice.org/
E-Mail: asgelect@samoatelco.com and *info@eo.as.gov*
684/699-3570 and 684/699-3571   FAX 684/699-3574

-Candidates on Ballot
-Election Results
-Federal Campaign Finance Reports
   (Online via FEC.gov)
-Federal Personal Financial Reports
-Territorial Campaign Finance Reports

LEGISLATIVE REFERENCE

Nathaniel Savali, Director
Legislative Reference Bureau
Legislature of American Samoa
P.O. Box 485
Pago Pago, American Samoa 96799
684/633-5233

DEPARTMENT OF COMMERCE

Alex Zodiacal, Manager
Economic Development Division
Department of Commerce
A.P. Lutali Executive Office Building, 2nd Floor
Utulei, American Samoa 96799
URL http://doc.as.gov/economic-development/business/
684/633-5155   FAX 684/633-4195

-Business Licensing

ATTORNEY GENERAL

Talauega Eleasalo V. Ale (Appointed)
Attorney General of American Samoa
Executive Office Building, 3rd Floor
P.O. Box 7
Pago Pago, American Samoa 96799
E-Mail: LA@as.gov
684/633-4163 and 684/633-7504   FAX 684/633-1838

   Mitzie Jessop, Deputy Attorney General
   E-Mail: mitzie.jessop@la.as.gov

-Other Court Actions

ARIZONA

SECRETARY OF STATE

Michele Reagan (Elected, R)
Secretary of State
State Capitol, Executive Tower, 7th Floor
1700 West Washington Street
Phoenix, Arizona 85007-2808
URL http://www.azsos.gov
E-Mail: sosadmin@azsos.gov
602/542-0681 FAX 602/542-1575

    Lee Miller, Deputy Secretary of State
        E-Mail: lmiller@azsos.gov
        602/542-4919 FAX 602/542-1575
    Eric Spencer, State Election Director
        E-Mail: espencer@azsos.gov
        602/542-6167 FAX 602/542-6172
    Scott Cancelosi, Director of Public Services
        E-Mail: scancelosi@azsos.gov
        602/542-0223 FAX 602/542-6187
    Bill Maaske, Chief Information Officer
        E-Mail: bmaaske@azsos.gov
        602/926-3603 FAX 602/542-1575
    Pat Viverto, Director of Business Services
        E-Mail: pvtverto@azsos.gov
        602/542-3060 FAX 602/542-4366
    Matt Roberts, Director of Communications
        E-Mail: mroberts@azsos.gov
        602/542-2228 FAX 602/542-1575
    Liz Atkinson, Chief Financial Officer
        E-Mail: latkinson@azsos.gov
        602/542-6171 FAX 602/542-1575

-Candidates on Ballot
-Election Results
-Federal Campaign Finance Reports
    (Online via FEC.gov)
-Federal Personal Financial Reports
-State Campaign Finance Reports
-State Personal Financial Reports
-State Lobby Reports
-State Initiative/Referendum Spending Reports
-Voting Accessibility

CITIZENS CLEAN ELECTIONS COMMISSION

Mitchell C. Laird, Chair
Citizens Clean Elections Commission
1616 West Adams, Suite 110
Phoenix, Arizona 85007
URL http://www.azcleanelections.gov
602/364-3477 FAX 602/364-3487
1-877/631-8891 (Toll Free)

    Steve M. Titla, Commissioner
    Damien R. Meyer, Commissioner
    Mark S. Kimble, Commissioner
    Galen D. Paton, Commissioner

    Thomas M. Collins, Executive Director
        E-Mail: thomas.collins@azcleanelections.gov
    Paula Thomas, Executive Officer
        E-Mail: paula.thomas@azcleanelections.gov
    Sara Larsen, Financial Affairs and Compliance Officer
        E-Mail: sara.larsen@azcleanelections.gov
    Gina Roberts, Voter Education Manager
        E-Mail: gina.roberts@azcleanelections.gov
    Mike Becker, Policy Director
        E-Mail: mike.becker@azcleanelections.gov
    Alec Shaffer, Executive Support Specialist
        E-Mail: alec.shaffer@azcleanelections.gov

-Full Public Funding to Statewide and Legislative
    Candidates
-Candidate Statement Pamphlet
-Voter Education
-Sponsorship of Candidate Debates
-Regulation of Campaign Finance Reports

CORPORATION COMMISSION

Patricia Barfield, Director	* -Corporate Registration and Records
Corporations Division	* -Limited Liability Company Registration
Corporation Commission	* -Name Reservations
1300 West Washington Street, First Floor	*
Phoenix, Arizona 85007	*
URL http://www.azcc.gov	*
E-Mail: mailmaster@azcc.gov	*
602/542-3026 FAX 602/542-0900	*
	*
Corporate Filing Section	*
602/542-3026 FAX 602/542-4100	*
Annual Report Filing Information	*
602/542-3285 FAX 602/542-0082	*
Corporate Records Section	*
602/542-3026 FAX 602/542-3414	*

NAVAJO NATION ETHICS AND RULES OFFICE

	*
Vernon J. Roanhorse, Executive Director	* -Administrative Hearings
Navajo Nation Ethics and Rules Office	* -Ethics Clearance
P.O. Box 5490	* -Standards of Conduct
Window Rock, Arizona 86515	* -Navajo Ethics in Government Law
URL http://www.nnethicsrules.navajo-nsn.gov	* -Investigations
928/871-6369 FAX 928/871-7168	* -Presentations on Ethics Law

LEGISLATIVE REFERENCE

	*
Michael E. Braun, Director	*
Legislative Council	*
State Capitol, Suite 100	*
1700 West Washington Street	*
Phoenix, Arizona 85007-2899	*
URL http://www.azleg.gov	*
E-Mail: mbraun@azleg.gov	*
602/926-4236 FAX 602/926-4803	*

ATTORNEY GENERAL

	*
Mark Brnovich (Elected, R)	* -Other Court Actions
Attorney General of Arizona	*
1275 West Washington Street	*
Phoenix, Arizona 85007-2926	*
URL http://www.azag.gov	*
E-Mail: aginfo@azag.gov	*
602/542-5025 FAX 602/542-4085	*
	*
John Lopez, Solicitor General	*
602/542-8986 FAX 602/542-8308	*
E-Mail: john.lopez@azag.gov	*

ARKANSAS

SECRETARY OF STATE

Mark Martin (Elected, R)
Secretary of State
256 State Capitol Building
Little Rock, Arkansas 72201
URL http://www.sos.arkansas.gov
501/682-1010 FAX 501/682-3510

Kelly Boyd
Chief Deputy Secretary of State
256 State Capitol Building
Little Rock, Arkansas 72201
E-Mail: kelly.boyd@sos.arkansas.gov
501/682-3401 FAX 501/682-1213

Leslie Bellamy
Interim Director of Elections
026 State Capitol Building
Little Rock, Arkansas 72201
E-Mail: leslie.bellamy@sos.arkansas.gov
501/682-5070 FAX 501/682-3408
1-800/482-1127 (Toll Free)

-Candidates on Ballot
-Election Results
-Federal Campaign Finance Reports
   (Online via FEC.gov)
-Federal Personal Financial Reports
-State Campaign Finance Reports
-State Personal Financial Reports
-State Lobby Reports

Kevin Niehaus
Director of Business and Commercial Services
1401 West Capitol, Suite 250
Little Rock, Arkansas 72201
501/682-3409 FAX 501/682-3437
1-888/233-0325 (Toll Free)

-Corporate Registration

ARKANSAS STATE BOARD OF ELECTION COMMISSIONERS

Justin Clay, Director
Arkansas State Board of Election Commissioners
501 Woodlane Avenue, Suite 401N
Little Rock, Arkansas 72201
URL http://www.arkansas.gov/sbec
E-Mail: clay.sbec@sos.arkansas.gov
501/682-1834 FAX 501/682-1782
1-800/411-6996 (Toll Free)

Gaye Swaim, Deputy Director
501/682-4578

Jon Davidson, Educational Services Manager
501/682-1856

-Develops Educational Resources for Candidates
   and County Election Administrators
-Develops Specialized Training Programs for
   County Election Administrators
-Monitors County Compliance with Federal and
   State Election Laws
-Investigates Allegations of Election Misconduct
   and Election Law Violations and Renders
   Reports of Findings
-Imposes Disciplinary Actions or Refers to the
   Proper Law Enforcement Authority
-Funds State-Supported Political Party Primary
   Elections, Nonpartisan Judicial General
   Elections, and Statewide Special Elections

ARKANSAS ETHICS COMMISSION

Graham F. Sloan, Director
Arkansas Ethics Commission
501 Woodlane Drive, Suite 301-N
Little Rock, Arkansas 72201
501/324-9600   FAX 501/324-9606

    Jill Rogers Barham, Staff Attorney
    Teresa Keathley, Director of Compliance
    Drew Blankenship, Director of Compliance

*
* -Issues Advisory Opinions and Provides Guidance
*   on Ethics Laws
* -Maintains Report Files on all Ballot Question and
*   Legislative Question Committees
* -Monitors Compliance with Disclosure
*   Requirements
* -Drafts, Reviews and Approves Disclosure Forms
* -Investigates Alleged Violations and Determines
*   Whether Violations have Occurred
* -Issues Disciplinary Actions or Refers Findings to a
*   Prosecuting Attorney

LEGISLATIVE REFERENCE

Marty Garrity, Director
Bureau of Legislative Research
Room 315, State Capitol
Little Rock, Arkansas 72201
URL http://www.arkleg.state.ar.us
501/682-1937   FAX 501/682-1936

ATTORNEY GENERAL

Leslie Rutledge (Elected, R)
Attorney General of Arkansas
323 Center Street, Suite 200
Little Rock, Arkansas 72201
URL http://www.arkansasag.gov
E-Mail: oag@arkansasag.gov
501/682-2007   FAX 501/682-8084
1-800/482-8982 (Toll Free)

* -Other Court Actions

CALIFORNIA

SECRETARY OF STATE

Alex Padilla (Elected, D)
Secretary of State
1500 11th Street
Sacramento, California 95814-2974
URL http://www.sos.ca.gov
916/653-7244   FAX 916/653-1458

    Bill Mabie, Chief Deputy Secretary of State
    Jacqueline Kinney, Assistant Chief Deputy and Counsel
    916/653-7244   FAX 916/651-8295

    Susan Lapsley, Deputy Secretary of State, Help America Vote Act
        Activities and Counsel
    916/653-7244   FAX 916/653-4620

Jana Lean, Chief
Elections Division
1500 11th Street, 5th Floor
Sacramento, California 95814-2974
E-Mail: Elections@sos.ca.gov
916/657-2166   FAX 916/653-3214
1-800/345-8683 (Toll Free)

-Candidates on Ballot
-Election Results
-Voting Accessibility
-Measures on Ballot
-Fraud Investigations
-Voter Registration and Outreach

Chris Reynolds, Chief
Political Reform Division
1500 11th Street, Room 495
Sacramento, California 95814-2974
URL http://CAL-ACCESS.sos.ca.gov
916/653-6224   FAX 916/653-5045

-State Campaign Registration and Disclosure
    Reports (Paper and Electronic)
-State Lobbying Registration and Disclosure
    Reports (Paper and Electronic)
-Electronic Lobbying Directory (Lobbyists,
    Lobbyist Employers and Lobbying Firms)
-Federal Personal Financial Reports
-State Personal Financial Reports

Business Entities Section
Business Programs Division
URL http://www.sos.ca.gov/business/be/
916/657-5448

-Corporate Registration

CALIFORNIA FAIR POLITICAL PRACTICES COMMISSION

Jodi Remke, Chair
California Fair Political Practices Commission
428 J Street, Suite 620
Sacramento, California 95814
URL http://www.fppc.ca.gov
916/322-5660
1-866/275-3772

-Economic Interest Reports
-Opinions on Compliance with the Political Reform
    Act
-Enforcement Responsibility for the Political
    Reform Act
-Anti-"Revolving Door" Prohibitions
-State Lobbyist Registration and Reports
-State and Local Campaign Finance Disclosure
-State Contribution Limits and Voluntary
    Expenditure Limits
-Gift Limits and Reporting

    Erin V. Peth, Executive Director
    Hyla P. Wagner, General Counsel
    John Wallace, Assistant General Counsel
    Galena West, Chief, Enforcement Division
    Dave Brainbridge, Assistant Chief, Enforcement Division
    Loressa Hon, Chief, Administration Division
    (Vacant), Chief, External Affairs and Education Division
    Jay Wierenga, Director, Communications
    Philip Ung, Director, Legislative and External Affairs
    Sheva Tabatabainejad, Commission Assistant

FRANCHISE TAX BOARD

Selvi Stanislaus, Executive Officer
California Franchise Tax Board
P.O. Box 115
Rancho Cordova, California 95741-0115
URL http://www.ftb.ca.gov
916/845-4543   FAX 916/845-3191

      Privacy, Disclosure and Data Resources Section
      ACD Line 916/845-6670   FAX 916/845-4849

-Random Audits of Campaign Finance Reports and
    Lobbyists, as Directed by the Fair Political
    Practices Commission

OFFICE OF LEGISLATIVE COUNSEL

Diane F. Boyer-Vine, Legislative Counsel
Office of Legislative Counsel
State Capitol, Suite 3021
Sacramento, California 95814
URL http://www.legislativecounsel.ca.gov
916/341-8000   FAX 916/341-8020

LOS ANGELES COUNTY REGISTRAR-RECORDER/COUNTY CLERK

Dean C. Logan, Registrar Recorder/County Clerk
Campaign Finance Section
12400 Imperial Highway, Room 2003
Norwalk, California 90650
URL http://www.lavote.net
562/462-2339   FAX 562/651-2548

-State Superior Court Judicial Annual/Candidate
    Form 700
-Candidate Form 700 For County and State Offices
-State Candidates Under $25,000 Threshold
-County Candidates and County General Purpose
    Committees and County Measures
-State Officeholder, State Candidate, State
    Measures, State Major Donors and State
    General Purpose Committees Prior To 2011

LOS ANGELES CITY ETHICS COMMISSION

Heather Holt, Executive Director
Los Angeles City Ethics Commission
200 North Spring Street
City Hall, 24th Floor
Los Angeles, California 90012
URL http://ethics.lacity.org
E-Mail: ethics.commission@lacity.org
213/978-1960   FAX 213/978-1988

-Administrative and Oversight Responsibility for
    Campaign Financing, Lobbying and
    Governmental Ethics Laws
-Disclosure Reports for Candidates, Ballot Measure
    Committees, Independent Expenditures and
    Officeholders
-Public Matching Funds Program
-Statements of Economic Interests for City Officials
-Lobbying Registration and Disclosure Reports
-Opinions and Formal and Informal Advice
-Training
-Whistleblower Hotline
-Audits and Investigations
-Administrative Enforcement
-Electronic Filings
-Searchable Online Disclosure Databases
-Policy Memoranda and Legislative
    Recommendations

SACRAMENTO COUNTY VOTER REGISTRATION AND ELECTIONS

Jill LaVine, Registrar of Voters
County of Sacramento Voter Registration and Elections
7000 65th Street, Suite A
Sacramento, California 95823-2315
E-Mail: lavinej@saccounty.net
916/875-6558 FAX 916/876-5130

-County Campaign Finance Reports

SAN FRANCISCO DEPARTMENT OF ELECTIONS

John Arntz, Director of Elections
Department of Elections
City and County of San Francisco
1 Dr. Carlton B. Goodlett Place, Room 48
San Francisco, California 94102
URL http://www.sfelections.org
E-Mail: sfvote@sfgov.org
415/554-4375 FAX 415/554-7344
TDD 415/554-4386

-Candidates and Measures on Ballot
-Election Results
-Statewide Campaign Finance Reports
-Voter Information and Services
-Voter Education and Outreach
-Voter Registration
-Usability of Voting Systems

SAN FRANCISCO ETHICS COMMISSION

Lee Ann Pelham, Executive Director
San Francisco Ethics Commission
25 Van Ness Avenue, Suite 220
San Francisco, California 94102-6053
URL http://www.sfethics.org
E-Mail: ethics.commission@sfgov.org
415/252-3100 FAX 415/252-3112

-City and County Campaign Finance Reports
-City and County Lobbyist Reports
-Campaign Consultant Reports
-Statements of Economic Interests for City Officials
 and Designated Employees
-Audit Reports of Candidate Committees and Local
 Ballot Measure Committees
-Advice Letters on Government Ethics-Related
 Matters
-Enforcement Responsibility for Lobbying,
 Campaign Finance and Ethics-Related Laws
-Public Financing Reports
-Electronic Filings

ATTORNEY GENERAL

Kamala D. Harris (Elected, D)
Attorney General of California
1300 I Street, Suite 1740
Sacramento, California 95814
URL http://oag.ca.gov
916/324-5437 FAX 916/323-5341
1-800/952-5225 (Toll Free)
    Mailing Address:
    P.O. Box 944255
    Sacramento, CA 94244-2550

Douglas J.Woods, Senior Assistant Attorney General
916/324-4663 FAX 916/324-8835

Ashley Johansson, Initiative Coordinator
916/445-4752 FAX 916/324-8835

-Proposed Initiative Measure Titles and Summaries
-Other Court Actions

SECRETARY OF STATE

Wayne Williams (Elected, R)
Secretary of State
1700 Broadway, Suite 250
Denver, Colorado 80290
URL http://www.sos.state.co.us
303/894-2200   FAX 303/869-4860
TDD 303/869-4867

Suzanne Staiert, Deputy Secretary of State

Judd Choate   -Candidates on Ballot
Director of Elections   -Election Results
1700 Broadway, Suite 200   -Federal Campaign Finance Reports
Denver, CO 80290   (Online via FEC.gov)
E-Mail: elections@sos.state.co.us   -Federal Personal Financial Reports
303/894-2200   FAX 303/869-4861   -State Campaign Finance Reports
                                                     -State Personal Financial Reports
Hilary Rudy, Deputy Director of Elections   -State Initiative/Referendum Spending Reports
Ben Schler, Legal Internal Operations Manager   -Voting Accessibility
Dwight Shellman, County and Regulation Support Manager
Melissa Polk, Legal Manager
Joel Albin, Ballot Access Manager
Stephen Bouey, Campaign Finance Manager
Minerva Padron, Voter Registration Manager
Vicky Stecklein, SCORE Program Manager

Angela Lawson, Program Manager   -State Lobby Reports
Lobbyist Registration Division
E-Mail: lobbyists@sos.state.co.us
303/894-2200 (ext. 6304)   FAX 303/869-4871

Mike Hardin, Director   -Business Registration
Business Division
E-Mail: business@sos.state.co.us
303/894-2200   FAX 303/869-4864

LEGISLATIVE REFERENCE

Mike Mauer, Director
Legislative Council
State Capitol Building, Room 029
Denver, Colorado 80203-1784
URL http://www.colorado.gov/cga-legislativecouncil
E-Mail: lcs.ga@state.co.us
303/866-3521 FAX 303/866-3855

ATTORNEY GENERAL

Cynthia Coffman (Elected, R)   -Other Court Actions
Attorney General of Colorado
Office of the Attorney General
Ralph L. Carr Colorado Judicial Center
1300 Broadway, Floor 10
Denver, Colorado 80203-5600
URL http://www.coag.gov
E-Mail: attorney.general@scoag.gov
720/508-6000   FAX 720/508-6030

CONNECTICUT

SECRETARY OF THE STATE

Denise W. Merrill (Elected, D)
Secretary of the State
30 Trinity Street
Hartford, Connecticut 06106
URL http://www.sots.ct.gov
860/509-6200 FAX 860/509-6209

James Field Spallone, Deputy Secretary of the State
30 Trinity Street
Hartford, Connecticut 06106
860/509-6212 FAX 860/509-6131

Peggy Reeves, Director
Legislation and Election Administration Division
30 Trinity Street
Hartford, Connecticut 06106
860/509-6100 FAX 860/509-6127
1-800/540-3764 (Toll Free in State)
TDD 1-800/303-3161

    Theodore Bromley, Staff Attorney
    Lewis A. Button, Staff Attorney
    Bernard Liu, Staff Attorney
    Heather Augeri, Elections Officer
    Joan Gibson, Elections Officer
    Shirley Surgeon, Elections Officer
    Pearl Williams, Elections Officer

Seth C. Klaskin, Director
Business Services Division
860/509-6003 FAX 860/509-6068
860/509-6002 (For Corporate Information)

-Candidates on Ballot
-Election Results
-Voter Registration
-Voting Accessibility
-Centralized Voter Registration System

-Business Registration

STATE ELECTIONS ENFORCEMENT COMMISSION

Michael J. Brandi, Executive Director and General Counsel
State Elections Enforcement Commission
20 Trinity Street
Hartford, Connecticut 06106-1628
URL http://www.ct.gov/seec
E-Mail: SEEC@ct.gov
860/256-2940 FAX 860/256-2983
1-866/733-2463 (Toll Free in CT)

    Shannon Keif, Legal Program Director
    Linda Waterman, Director, Campaign Disclosure and Audit Unit

-Federal Campaign Finance Reports
    (Online via FEC.gov)
-Federal Personal Financial Reports
-State Campaign Finance Reports
-Electronic Filings
-Enforcement of State Campaign Finance and
    Election Laws

OFFICE OF STATE ETHICS

Carol E. Carson, Executive Director
Office of State Ethics
18-20 Trinity Street, Suite 205
Hartford, Connecticut 06106-1660
URL http://www.ct.gov/ethics
E-Mail: ose@ct.gov
860/263-2400   FAX 860/263-2402

    Alaaeldin "Al" Ali, Information Technology Analyst
    Diane P. Buxo, Paralegal Specialist
    Marc Crayton, Assistant Ethics Enforcement Officer
    Taliea Hatcher-Redway, Clerk Typist
    Barbara Housen, General Counsel
    Malissa Hurry, Paralegal Specialist
    T.J. Jones, Ethics Enforcement Officer
    Jarrod Kosky, Assistant General Counsel
    Peter Lewandowski, Assistant General Counsel
    Ann Morgan, Information Technology Analyst
    Michael Morrissey, Legal Investigator
    Nancy Nicolescu, Director of Education and Communications
    Brian O'Dowd, Deputy General Counsel
    Mark Wasielewski, Assistant Ethics Enforcement Officer

-State Personal Financial Reports
-State Lobby Reports
-Enforcement of Ethics and Lobbying Laws
-Advisory and Staff Opinions

LEGISLATIVE REFERENCE

Stephanie A. D'Ambrose, Director
Office of Legislative Research
300 Capitol Avenue, Room 5300
Hartford, Connecticut 06106
URL http://www.cga.ct.gov/olr
E-Mail: stephanie.dambrose@cga.ct.gov
E-Mail: olr@cga.ct.gov
860/240-8400   FAX 860/240-8881

    Tracey Otero, Senior Supervisor and Webmaster
    E-Mail: tracey.otero@cga.ct.gov
    Kristin Sullivan, Chief Legislative Analyst
    E-Mail: kristin.sullivan@cga.ct.gov
    Terrance Adams, Associate Legislative Analyst
    E-Mail: terrance.adams@cga.ct.gov

-Bill Tracking
-Bill Analyses
-Legislative Library

ATTORNEY GENERAL

George Jepsen (Elected, D)
Attorney General of Connecticut
55 Elm Street
Hartford, Connecticut 06106
URL http://www.ct.gov/ag
E-Mail: Attorney.General@ct.gov
860/808-5318 FAX 860/808-5387
    Mailing Address:
    P.O. Box 120
    Hartford, Connecticut 06141-0120

    Mark F. Kohler, Department Head
    Assistant Attorney General
    Special Litigation Department
    860/808-5020 FAX 860/808-5347

*
*   -Other Court Actions
*
*
*
*
*
*
*
*
*
*
*
*
*

DELAWARE

SECRETARY OF STATE

Jeffrey W. Bullock (Appointed, D)
Secretary of State
Townsend Building
401 Federal Street, Suite 3
Dover, Delaware 19901
URL http://www.sos.delaware.gov
302/739-4111 FAX 302/739-3811

    Richard Geisenberger, Chief Deputy Secretary of State

April Wright, Corporations Administrator
Division of Corporations
URL http://www.corp.delaware.gov
302/739-4111 FAX 302/739-3811

-Federal Campaign Finance Reports
    (Online via FEC.gov)
-Federal Personal Financial Reports

-Corporate Registration

STATE ELECTION COMMISSIONER

Elaine Manlove
State Election Commissioner
905 South Governors Avenue, Suite 170
Dover, Delaware 19904
URL http://elections.delaware.gov
E-Mail: elaine.manlove@state.de.us
302/739-4277 FAX 302/739-6794

-Candidates on Ballot
-Election Results
-State Campaign Finance Reports
-Voting Accessibility

DELAWARE STATE PUBLIC INTEGRITY COMMISSION

Deborah J. Moreau, Esq.
Commission Counsel
Delaware State Public Integrity Commission
Margaret O'Neill Building
410 Federal Street, Suite 3 (Room 211)
Dover, Delaware 19901
URL http://www.depic.delaware.gov
E-Mail: deborah.moreau@state.de.us
302/739-2399 FAX 302/739-2398

-State Personal Financial Reports
    (Elected and Appointed Officials)
-State Lobby Reports

LEGISLATIVE REFERENCE

Lori Christiansen, Director
Division of Research
Legislative Council
411 Legislative Avenue
Dover, Delaware 19901
URL http://www.legis.delaware.gov
302/744-4114 FAX 302/739-3895
1-800/282-8545 (Toll Free in State)

ATTORNEY GENERAL

Matthew Denn (Elected, D)
Attorney General of Delaware
820 North French Street, 6th Floor
Wilmington, Delaware 19801
URL http://attorneygeneral.delaware.gov
E-Mail: Attorney.General@State.DE.US
302/577-8400   FAX 302/577-6630

*
*   -Other Court Actions
*
*
*
*
*
*

DISTRICT OF COLUMBIA

SECRETARY OF THE DISTRICT OF COLUMBIA

Lauren C. Vaughan (Appointed, D)
Secretary of the District of Columbia
1350 Pennsylvania Avenue, N.W., Suite 600
Washington, D.C. 20004
URL http://os.dc.gov
202/727-6306   FAX 202/727-3582

BOARD OF ELECTIONS

Terri Stroud, Acting Executive Director
Board of Elections
One Judiciary Square
441 Fourth Street, N.W., Suite 250 North
Washington, D.C. 20001-2745
URL http://www.dcboee.org
E-Mail: director@dcboee.org
202/727-2525   FAX 202/347-2648
TDD 202/639-8916

    Sylvia Goldsberry-Adams, Operations Manager
    Kenneth J. McGhie, General Counsel
    Margarita Mikhaylova, Acting Public Affairs Specialist

-Candidates on Ballot
-Election Results
-Voting Accessibility
-Voter Registration
-Centralized Voter Registration System
-Measures on Ballot

OFFICE OF CAMPAIGN FINANCE

Cecily E. Collier-Montgomery, Director of Campaign Finance
Office of Campaign Finance
Frank D. Reeves Municipal Building
2000 14th Street, N.W., Suite 433
Washington, D.C. 20009
URL http://ocf.dc.gov
E-Mail: ocf@dc.gov
202/671-0547 or 202/671-0550   FAX 202/671-0658

    Renee Coleman-Rollins, Audit Manager
    S. Wesley Williams, Public Affairs Manager
    William Sanford, General Counsel

-District Campaign Finance Reports
-District Initiative/Referendum Spending Reports
-District Initiative/Referendum/Recall/Charter
    Amendment Committee Reports
-District Constituent Service and Statehood
    Fund Reports
-Electronic Filings
-Legal Defense Fund Reports
-District Inaugural/Transition Committee Reports

BOARD OF ETHICS AND GOVERNMENT ACCOUNTABILITY

Darrin P. Sobin, Esq., Director
Office of Government Ethics
441 4th Street, N.W., Suite 830 South
Washington, D.C. 20001
URL http://www.bega-dc.gov
E-Mail: darrin.sobin@dc.gov
202/481-3411, Hotline: 202/535-1002

-District Financial Disclosure Reports
-District Lobby Reports
-Ethics Advice and Advisory Opinions

Traci L. Hughes, Esq., Director
Office of Open Government
441 4th Street N.W., Suite 540 South
Washington, D.C. 20001
URL http://www.bega-dc.gov
E-Mail:traci.hughes@dc.gov
202/481-3406

-FOIA Compliance
-Open Meetings Act Compliance
-Advisory Opinions

DEPARTMENT OF CONSUMER AND REGULATORY AFFAIRS

Melinda M. Bolling, Interim Director
Department of Consumer and Regulatory Affairs
1100 4th Street, S.W.
Washington, D.C. 20024
URL http://dcra.dc.gov
E-Mail: dcra@dc.gov
202/442-4400 FAX 202/442-9445

*
*
* -Corporate Registration
* -Business Licensing
* -Construction Permits
* -Property Inspections
*
*
*

LEGISLATIVE REFERENCE

Nyasha Smith
Secretary to the Council
Council of the District of Columbia
1350 Pennsylvania Avenue, N.W., Room 5
Washington, D.C. 20004
URL http://www.dccouncil.us
202/724-8080 FAX 202/347-3070

ATTORNEY GENERAL

Karl A. Racine (Elected, D)
Attorney General
One Judiciary Square
441 4th Street N.W., Suite 1100 South
Washington, D.C. 20001
URL http://oag.dc.gov
E-Mail: dc.oag@dc.gov
202/727-3400 FAX 202/347-8922

*
* -Other Court Actions
*
*
*
*
*
*
*

SECRETARY OF STATE

Kenneth Detzner (Appointed, R)
Secretary of State
500 South Bronough Street
Tallahassee, Florida 32399-0250
URL http://dos.myflorida.com
E-Mail:secretaryofstate@DOS.MyFlorida.com
850/245-6500 FAX 850/245-6125

    Jennifer Kennedy, Assistant Secretary of State
    John Boynton, Deputy Secretary for Administrative Services,
        Corporations and Elections

Maria Matthews, Esq., Director
Division of Elections
500 South Bronough Street
R.A. Gray Building, Room 316
Tallahassee, Florida 32399-0250
URL http://dos.myflorida.com/elections
E-Mail: DivElections@DOS.MyFlorida.com
850/245-6200 FAX 850/245-6217, 850/245-6218

    Gary J. Holland, Assistant Division Director
    Kristi Bronson, Bureau Chief of Election Records
    Toshia Brown, Bureau Chief of Voting Registration Services
    Linda Hastings-Ard, Bureau Chief of Voting Systems

- Candidates and Issues on Ballot
- Election Results and Statistics
- Federal Campaign Finance Reports
  (Online via FEC.gov)
- State Campaign Finance Reports for Candidates
  and Political Entities
- State Initiatives/Referendums
- Third-Party Voter Registration Organizations
  Registrations
- Voting Accessibility
- Electronic Filing Database
- Electronic Filings

Brenda L. Vorisek, Director
Division of Corporations
2661 Executive Center Circle
Clifton Building
Tallahassee, Florida 32301
URL http://www.sunbiz.org
E-Mail: Brenda.Vorisek@DOS.MyFlorida.com
850/245-6000

- Business Entity Filing/Registration Information
  (Current Status, Principal Officers/Directors/
  Managers, Principal Office and/or
  Mailing Address)
- Document Images Available for Download

FLORIDA COMMISSION ON ETHICS

Virlindia Doss, Executive Director
Florida Commission on Ethics
325 John Knox Road, Building E, Suite 200
Tallahassee, Florida 32303
URL http://www.ethics.state.fl.us
E-Mail: doss.virlindia@leg.state.fl.us
850/488-7864 FAX 850/488-3077
    Mailing Address:
    P.O. Drawer 15709
    Tallahassee, Florida 32317-5709

    C. Christopher Anderson, III, General Counsel and Deputy
       Executive Director
    Millie Fulford, Complaint Coordinator
    Kerrie J. Stillman, Director of Operations and Communications

- Administration of Disclosure of Financial Interests
- Gift Disclosure Forms Other Than Those of
  Legislative Members and Staff
- Investigative Complaints of Breaches of the
  Public Trust by Public Officers and
  Employees
- Render Legally Binding Advisory Opinions
  Interpreting the Ethics Laws

FLORIDA ELECTIONS COMMISSION

Amy McKeever Toman, Executive Director
Florida Elections Commission
107 West Gaines Street
Collins Building, Suite 224
Tallahassee, Florida 32399-1050
URL http://www.fec.state.fl.us
850/922-4539   FAX 850/921-0783

    Eric Lipman, General Counsel
    Stephanie Cunningham, Assistant General Counsel
    Donna Malphurs, Agency Clerk

-Enforcement of State Elections Laws

LEGISLATIVE REFERENCE

Lobbyist Registration Office
Division of Legislative Information Services
Office of Legislative Services
111 West Madison Street, Room G-68
Tallahassee, Florida 32399-1425
URL https://floridalobbyist.gov
850/922-4990   FAX 850/921-5345

-Legislative and Executive Branch Lobbyist
    Registration
-Compensation Reports
-Gift Disclosure Forms
    (Legislative Members and Staff)

ATTORNEY GENERAL

Pam Bondi (Elected, R)
Florida Attorney General
The Capitol, PL-01
Tallahassee, Florida 32399-1050
URL http://www.myfloridalegal.com
850/414-3300   FAX 850/410-1630
850/414-3990 (Citizens Services)
1-866/966-7226 (Toll Free in State)

-Other Court Actions

GEORGIA

SECRETARY OF STATE

Brian P. Kemp (Elected, R)
Secretary of State
214 State Capitol
Atlanta, Georgia 30334
URL http://www.sos.ga.gov
E-Mail: sos@sos.ga.gov
404/656-2881   FAX 678/717-5757

    Tim Fleming, Deputy Secretary of State
    Robin Herron, Executive Assistant

Chris Harvey, Director
Elections Division
Suite 802, West Tower
2 Martin Luther King, Jr. Drive, S.E.
Atlanta, Georgia 30334-1505
E-Mail: elections@sos.ga.gov
404/656-2871   FAX 404/232-1863
TDD 404/656-1787

    Jessica Simmons, Assistant Elections Director
    Ryan Germany, Legal Counsel

-Candidates on Ballot
-Election Results
-Voting Accessibility
-State Campaign Finance Reports Filed Prior to 2006

Shawnzia Thomas, Director
Corporations Division
Suite 313, West Tower
2 Martin Luther King, Jr. Drive, S.E.
Atlanta, Georgia 30334-1505
404/657-2817   FAX 404/657-1876

-Corporate Registration

GOVERNMENT TRANSPARENCY AND CAMPAIGN FINANCE COMMISSION

Stefan Ritter, Executive Secretary
Georgia Government Transparency and Campaign Finance Commission
200 Piedmont Avenue, S.E.
Suite 1402, West Tower
Atlanta, Georgia 30334
URL http://www.ethics.ga.gov
E-Mail: gaethics@ethics.ga.gov
404/463-1980   FAX 404/463-1988

-Federal Campaign Finance Reports
    (Online via FEC.gov)
-Federal Personal Financial Reports
-State Campaign Finance Reports
-State Personal Financial Reports
-State Campaign Finance Disclosure Enforcement
-State Personal Financial Disclosure Enforcement
-State Lobbyist Reports
-State Lobbyist Registration
-City/County Lobbyist Reports
-Vendor Gift Disclosure Reports and Enforcement
-Vendor Lobbyist Disclosure
-Electronic Filings

LEGISLATIVE REFERENCE

Angie Fiese, Acting Director
Senate Research Office
204 Coverdell Legislative Office Building
Atlanta, Georgia 30334
URL http://www.senate.ga.gov/sro/en-US/Home.aspx
E-Mail: Angie.Fiese@senate.ga.gov
404/656-0015 FAX 404/657-0929

Jennifer Yarber, Director
Senate Press Office
201 Coverdell Legislative Office Building
Atlanta, GA 30334
E-Mail: Jennifer.yarber@senate.ga.gov
404/656-0028 FAX 404/657-0929
1-800/282-5803 (Toll Free)

Melody DeBussey, Director
Senate Budget and Evaluation Office
208 Coverdell Legislative Office Building
Atlanta, Georgia 30334
URL: http://www.senate.ga.gov/sbeo/en-US/Home.aspx
E-Mail· melody.debussey@senate.ga.gov
404/463-1970 FAX 404/463-0346

    Brent Churchwell, Deputy Director
    E-Mail: brent.churchwell@senate.ga.gov

Martha Wigton, Director
House Budget and Research Office
412 Coverdell Legislative Office Building
Atlanta, Georgia 30334
URL http://www.legis.ga.gov
E-Mail: martha.wigton@house.ga.gov
404/656-5050 FAX 404/657-8349

    Christine Murdock, Deputy Director
    E-Mail: christine.murdock@house.ga.gov

Betsy Lynch, Director
House Media Services
205-J Coverdell Legislative Office Building
Atlanta, Georgia 30334
URL http://www.house.ga.gov/mediaservices
E-Mail: betsy.lynch@house.ga.gov
404/656-3996

ATTORNEY GENERAL

Samuel S. Olens (Elected, R)   -All Court Actions
Attorney General of Georgia
40 Capitol Square, S.W.
Atlanta, Georgia 30334-1300
URL http://law.ga.gov
404/656-3300 FAX 404/657-8733

GUAM

LIEUTENANT GOVERNOR

Raymond S. Tenorio (Elected, R)
Lieutenant Governor
R.J. Bordallo Governor's Complex
P.O. Box 2950
Hagatna, Guam 96932
URL http://www.lt.guam.gov
671/475-9380   FAX 671/477-2007

ELECTION COMMISSION

Maria I.D. Pangelinan, Executive Director
Guam Election Commission
2nd Floor, Suite 200
414 West Soledad Avenue, GCIC Building
Hagatna, Guam 96910
URL http://www.gec.guam.gov
E-Mail: vote@gec.guam.gov
671/477-9791   FAX 671/477-1895

-Candidates on Ballot
-Election Results
-Federal Campaign Finance Reports
-Federal Personal Financial Reports
-Territorial Campaign Finance Reports

DEPARTMENT OF REVENUE AND TAXATION

Tammy Asuncion, License Officer
General Licensing and Registration
Regulatory Division
Department of Revenue and Taxation
1240 Army Drive
Barrigada, Guam 96913
URL https://www.guamtax.com/about/regulatory.html
E-Mail: tammy.asuncion@revtax.guam.gov
671/635-1829, 635-7670   FAX 671/633-2643
   Mailing Address:
   P.O. Box 23607
   GMF, Guam 96921

-Corporate Registration

LEGISLATIVE REFERENCE

Vince P. Arriola, Executive Director
Guam Legislature
155 Hessler Place
Hagatna, Guam 96910
URL http://www.guamlegislature.org
E-Mail: vparriola1@gmail.com
671/472-7679   FAX 671/472-3459

ATTORNEY GENERAL

Elizabeth Barrett-Anderson (Elected)
Attorney General
Office of the Attorney General of Guam
590 South Marine Corps Drive
ITC Building, Suite 706
Tamuning, Guam 96913
URL http://www.guamag.org
E-Mail: law@guamag.org
671/475-3324, 475-3406, and 475-3360   FAX 671/472-2493

Philip J. Tydingco, Chief Deputy Attorney General

*
*   -Other Court Actions
*
*
*
*
*
*
*
*
*

LIEUTENANT GOVERNOR

Shan S. Tsutsui (Elected, D)
Lieutenant Governor
State Capitol, 5th Floor
415 South Beretania Street
Honolulu, Hawaii 96813
URL http://www.hawaii.gov/ltgov
E-Mail: ltgov@hawaii.gov
808/586-0255   FAX 808/586-0231

OFFICE OF ELECTIONS

Scott T. Nago, Chief Election Officer
Office of Elections
802 Lehua Avenue
Pearl City, Hawaii 96782
URL http://www.elections.hawaii.gov
E-Mail: elections@hawaii.gov
808/453-8683   FAX 808/453-6006
1-800/442-8683 (Neighbor Islands)

-Candidates on Ballot
-Election Results
-Voting Accessibility
-Voter Information and Referral Services

CAMPAIGN SPENDING COMMISSION

Kristin E. Izumi-Nitao, Executive Director
Campaign Spending Commission
235 South Beretania Street, Room 300
Honolulu, Hawaii 96813
URL http://ags.hawaii.gov/campaign
808/586-0285   FAX 808/586-0288

    Tony Baldomero, Associate Director
    Gary K. Kam, General Counsel

-Federal Campaign Finance Reports
    (Online via FEC.gov)
-State Campaign Finance Reports
-State Public Financing Documentation
-Electronic Filings

STATE ETHICS COMMISSION

Susan D. Yoza, Associate Director
State Ethics Commission
ASB Tower, Suite 970
1001 Bishop Street
Honolulu, Hawaii 96813
URL http://ethics.hawaii.gov
E-Mail: ethics@hawaiiethics.org
808/587-0460   FAX 808/587-0470

-State Personal Financial Reports (State Officials
    and Candidates for State Elective Office)
-Gifts Disclosure Reports (State Officials)
-State Lobby Reports
-State Lobbying Laws
-Ethics Laws for State Government Officials

OFFICE OF INFORMATION PRACTICES

Cheryl Kakazu Park, Director
Office of Information Practices
No. 1 Capitol District Building, Suite 107
250 South Hotel Street
Honolulu, HI 96813
URL http://oip.hawaii.gov
E-Mail: oip@hawaii.gov
808/586-1400   FAX 808/586-1412

-Freedom of Information
-Sunshine Law (Open Meetings)

DEPARTMENT OF COMMERCE AND CONSUMER AFFAIRS

Ty Nohara, Commissioner of Securities
Business Registration Division
335 Merchant Street, Room 201
Honolulu, Hawaii 96813
URL http://cca.hawaii.gov/breg
808/586-2744 FAX 808/586-2733
808/587-1234 (Information Line)
    Mailing Address:
    P.O. Box 40
    Honolulu, Hawaii 96810

-Corporate Registration
-Securities Industry Regulation

LEGISLATIVE REFERENCE BUREAU

Charlotte Carter-Yamauchi, Director
Hawaii Legislative Reference Bureau
415 South Beretania Street, Room 446
Honolulu, Hawaii 96813
URL http://lrbhawaii.org
E-Mail: yamauchi@capitol.hawaii.gov
808/587-0666 FAX 808/587-0681

-Reports and Studies in Response to Legislative
  Requests
-Bill and Committee Report Drafting
-Statute Revision
-Legislative Reference Bureau Systems
-Legislative Library and Public Access Room
-Review of Administrative Agency Rules

DEPARTMENT OF TAXATION

Maria E. Zielinski, Director of Taxation
Department of Taxation
P.O. Box 259
Honolulu, Hawaii 96809-0259
URL http://tax.hawaii.gov
E-Mail: tax.directors.office@hawaii.gov
808/587-1540 FAX 808/587-1560

-Collection of Public Financing Funds

DEPARTMENT OF BUDGET AND FINANCE

Wesley Machida
Director of Finance
Department of Budget and Finance
250 South Hotel Street, Room 305
Honolulu, Hawaii 96813
URL http://budget.hawaii.gov/
E-Mail: hi.budgetandfinance@hawaii.gov
808/586-1518 FAX 808/586-1976
    Mailing Address:
    P.O. Box 150
    Honolulu, Hawaii 96810-0150

-Administration of Public Financing System

ATTORNEY GENERAL

Douglas S. Chin (Appointed, D)
Attorney General of Hawaii
425 Queen Street
Honolulu, Hawaii 96813
URL http://ag.hawaii.gov/
E-Mail: hawaiiag@hawaii.gov
808/586-1500 FAX 808/586-1239

-Other Court Actions

SECRETARY OF STATE

Lawrence Denney (Elected, R)
Secretary of State
700 West Jefferson, Room E-205
P.O. Box 83720
Boise, Idaho 83720-0080
URL http://www.sos.idaho.gov
208/334-2300 FAX 208/334-2080

    Tim Hurst, Chief Deputy Secretary of State

Betsie Kimbrough, Election Director
Elections Division
E-Mail: elections@sos.idaho.gov
208/334-2852 FAX 208/334-2282

Corporations Division
208/334-2301 FAX 208/334-2080

*
* -Candidates on Ballot
* -Election Results
* -Federal Campaign Finance Reports
*   (Online via FEC.gov)
* -Federal Personal Financial Reports
* -State Campaign Finance Reports
* -State Lobby Reports
* -State Initiative/Referendum Spending Reports
* -Distribution of Public Financing Funds
* -Voting Accessibility
* -Corporate Registration

IDAHO STATE CONTROLLER

Brandon Woolf (Elected, R)
State Controller and Secretary, Board of Examiners
700 West State Street, 5th Floor
P.O. Box 83720
Boise, Idaho 83720-0011
URL http://www.sco.idaho.gov
208/334-3100 FAX 208/334-2671

*
* -Membership on the Board of Canvassers
* -Maintenance of All Accounting and Financial
*   Records
* -Operation of the State's Computer Service Center
* -Annual State Financial Report

LEGISLATIVE REFERENCE

Legislative Reference Library
700 West Jefferson Street
P.O. Box 83720
Boise, Idaho 83720-0054
URL http://www.legislature.idaho.gov
208/334-2475 FAX 208/334-2125

ATTORNEY GENERAL

Lawrence G. Wasden (Elected, R)
Attorney General of Idaho
700 West Jefferson Street, Suite 210
P.O. Box 83720
Boise, Idaho 83720-0010
URL http://www.ag.idaho.gov
208/334-2400 FAX 208/854-8071

*
* -Other Court Actions

ILLINOIS

SECRETARY OF STATE

Jesse White (Elected, D)
Secretary of State
213 State Capitol
Springfield, Illinois 62756
URL http://www.cyberdriveillinois.com
217/782-2201 FAX 217/785-0358
1-800/252-8980 (Toll Free in State)

David Weisbaum, Director, Index Department
111 East Monroe Street
Springfield, Illinois 62756
E-Mail: dweisbaum@ilsos.net
217/782-7017 FAX 217/524-0930

-State Employee Economic Interest Statements
-State Lobbyist, Registration and Expenditure
   Reports

Ray Cachares, Director, Business Services Department
501 South Second Street, Suite 350
Springfield, Illinois 62756
217/782-6961

-Corporate LLC Registration, UCC Online Filings

STATE BOARD OF ELECTIONS

Steven S. Sandvoss, Executive Director
Illinois State Board of Elections
2329 South MacArthur Boulevard
Springfield, Illinois 62704-4503
URL http://www.elections.il.gov
E-Mail: ssandvoss@elections.il.gov
217/782-4141 FAX 217/782-5959

Candidates on Ballot
-Election Results
-Federal Campaign Finance Reports
   (Online via FEC.gov)
-Federal Personal Financial Reports
-State Campaign Finance Reports
-State Initiative/Referendum Spending Reports
-Voting Accessibility
-Electronic Filings

   Cris Cray, Legislative Liaison
      E-Mail: ccray@elections.il.gov
   Brent Davis, Director/Election Operations
      E-Mail: bdavis@elections.il.gov
   Becky Glazier, Special Projects Manager
      E-Mail: bglazier@elections.il.gov
   Jeremy Kirk, Director/Administrative Services
      E-Mail: jkirk@elections.il.gov
   Tom Newman, Director/Campaign Disclosure
      E-Mail: tnewman@elections.il.gov
   Kyle Thomas, Director/Voting and Registration Systems
      E-Mail: kthomas@elections.il.gov
   Kevin Turner, Director/Information Technology
      E-Mail: kturner@elections.il.gov

Jim Tenuto, Assistant Executive Director
Illinois State Board of Elections
100 West Randolph Street, Suite 14-100
Chicago, Illinois 60601
E-Mail: jtenuto@elections.il.gov
312/814-6440 FAX 312/814-6485

   Ken Menzel, General Counsel
      E-Mail: kmenzel@elections.il.gov
   Andy Nauman, Deputy Director of Campaign Disclosure
      E-Mail: anauman@elections.il.gov

LEGISLATIVE REFERENCE BUREAU

James W. Dodge, Executive Director
Legislative Reference Bureau
State Capitol Building, Room 112
Springfield, Illinois 62706
URL http://www.ilga.gov/commission/lrb_home.html
217/782-6625   FAX 217/785-4583

COOK COUNTY CLERK

David Orr (Elected, D)
Cook County Clerk
69 West Washington Street, Suite 500
Chicago, Illinois 60602
URL http://www.cookcountyclerk.com
E-Mail: d.orr@cookcountyil.gov
312/603-5656   FAX 312/603-9788
TTY 312/603-0902

-Candidates on Ballot
-Election Results
-Absentee Balloting
-Election Judges
-Voting Accessibility
-Statements of Economic Interest
-Cook County Lobbyist Registrations
    and Expenditure Reports

Noah Praetz, Director of Elections
Cook County Elections Department
URL http://www.cookcountyclerk.com
E-Mail: noah.praetz@cookcountyil.gov
312/603-0942   FAX 312/603-9786

Phillis Laster, Manager
Cook County Elections Department - Ethics Unit
E-Mail: clerk.ethics@cookcountyil.gov
312/603-1121   FAX 312/603-9787

COOK COUNTY BOARD OF ETHICS

Ranjit Hakim, Executive Director
Cook County Board of Ethics
69 West Washington Street, Suite 3040
Chicago, Illinois 60602-3007
URL http://www.cookcountyil.gov/ethics-board-of
E-Mail: cookcounty.ethics@cookcountyil.gov
312/603-4304   FAX 312/603-9988
TTY 312/603-1101

-Advisory Opinions
-Investigations and Hearings
-Audit Campaign Disclosures
-Ethics Training

    Kisha Johns, Executive Assistant
    312/603-1100   FAX 312/603-9988

CITY OF CHICAGO BOARD OF ELECTION COMMISSIONERS

Lance Gough, Executive Director
Board of Election Commissioners for the City of Chicago
69 West Washington Street, Suite 800
Chicago, Illinois 60602
URL http://www.chicagoelections.com
E-Mail: cboe@chicagoelections.net
312/269-7857
TTY 312/269-0027   FAX 312/269-0003

-Candidates on Ballot
-Election Results
-Voter Registration
-Sample Ballots
-Early and Absentee Voting
-Accessibility Services

CITY OF CHICAGO BOARD OF ETHICS

Steven I. Berlin, Executive Director
Chicago Board of Ethics
740 North Sedgwick Avenue, Suite 500
Chicago, Illinois 60654
URL http://www.cityofchicago.org/ethics
Email: sberlin@cityofchicago.org
312/742-8152   FAX 312/744-2793
TTY 312/744-5996

    Jef Johnson, Public Information Officer

*
*   -City Statements of Financial Interests for Officials,
*   Candidates and Employees Required to File
*   -List of Registered Lobbyists
*   -City Lobbyist Reports
*
*
*
*
*
*

ATTORNEY GENERAL

Lisa Madigan (Elected, D)
Attorney General of Illinois
500 South Second Street
Springfield, Illinois 62706
URL http://www.illinoisattorneygeneral.gov
E-Mail: attorney_general@state.il.us
217/782-1090   FAX 217/785-2551
TTY 877/844-5461

    Chicago Office:
    100 West Randolph Street, 12th Floor
    Chicago, Illinois 60601
    312/814-3000   FAX 312/814-3806
    TTY 800/964-3013

*
*   -Other Court Actions
*
*
*
*
*
*
*
*
*
*
*
*

INDIANA

SECRETARY OF STATE

Connie Lawson (Elected, R) Secretary of State State House, Room 201 200 West Washington Street Indianapolis, Indiana 46204 *URL http://www.in.gov/sos* 317/232-6536 FAX 317/233-3283	*

Brandon Clifton, Deputy Secretary of State
Valerie Warycha, Deputy Chief of Staff,
    Director of Communications and Media Contact

Business Services Division — -Corporate Registration
302 West Washington Street, Room E-018
Indianapolis, Indiana 46204
317/232-6576   FAX 317/233-3283

Securities Division
302 West Washington Street, Room E-111
Indianapolis, Indiana 46204
317/232-6681   FAX 317/233-3675

INDIANA ELECTION DIVISION

J. Bradley King, Co-Director
Angela M. Nussmeyer, Co-Director
Indiana Election Division
Office of the Secretary of State
302 West Washington Street, Room E-204
Indianapolis, Indiana 46204-2767
URL http://www.in.gov/sos/elections
E-Mail: elections@iec.in.gov
317/232-3939   FAX 317/233-6793
1-800/622-4941 (Toll Free in State)

-Candidates on Ballot
-Election Results
-Federal Campaign Finance Reports
    (Online via FEC.gov)
-Federal Personal Financial Reports
-State Campaign Finance Reports
-Electronic Filings
-Voting Accessibility

Abbey Taylor, Campaign Finance Coordinator
Michelle Thompson, Campaign Finance Coordinator
URL http://campaignfinance.in.gov

INDIANA OFFICE OF INSPECTOR GENERAL

Cynthia Carrasco, Inspector General
Indiana Office of Inspector General
315 West Ohio Street, Room 104
Indianapolis, Indiana 46202
URL http://www.in.gov/ig
317/232-3850   FAX 317/232-0707

-State Personal Financial Reports
    (Statewide Elected Officers and Candidates)
Criminal Ethics and Efficiency Issues

INDIANA LOBBY REGISTRATION COMMISSION

Charles Harris, Executive Director and General Counsel
Indiana Lobby Registration Commission
10 West Market Street, Suite 2940
Indianapolis, Indiana 46204-1927
URL http://www.in.gov/ilrc
E-Mail: charris@lrc.in.gov
317/232-9860   FAX 317/233-0077

      Amy Nicholson, Assistant Director
      Kaytie Barrett, Office Administrator

-State Legislative Lobbying Expenditure Reports
-State Legislative Lobbying Gift or Purchase
    Reporting
-Electronic Filings
-Public Record Holder

LEGISLATIVE REFERENCE

M. Caroline Spotts, Principal Clerk of the House
Indiana House of Representatives
State House, Room 3A-8
200 West Washington Street
Indianapolis, Indiana 46204-2786
URL http://iga.in.gov
317/232-9608

-Statements of Economic Interest for Incumbents
    and Candidates for State Representative

Jennifer L. Mertz, Principal Secretary of the Senate
Indiana State Senate
State House, Room 3A-North
200 West Washington Street
Indianapolis, Indiana 46204-2785
URL http://iga.in.gov
E-Mail: jennifer.mertz@iga.in.gov
317/232-9421

-Statements of Economic Interest for Incumbents
    and Candidates for State Senate

Legislative Services Agency
Legislative Information Center
State House, Room 301
200 West Washington Street
Indianapolis, Indiana 46204-2789
URL http://iga.in.gov
317/232-9856

-Senate and House Legislators' Statements of
    Economic Interest

ATTORNEY GENERAL

Greg Zoeller (Elected, R)
Attorney General of Indiana
Government Center South, 5th Floor
302 West Washington Street
Indianapolis, Indiana 46204
URL http://www.in.gov/attorneygeneral
317/232-6201   FAX 317/232-7979

-Other Court Actions

SECRETARY OF STATE

Paul D. Pate (Elected, R)
Secretary of State, Commissioner of Elections, State Registrar of Voters
Chairperson, Voter Registration Commission
Statehouse
Des Moines, Iowa 50319
URL http://sos.iowa.gov
E-Mail: sos@sos.iowa.gov
515/281-6230   FAX 515/242-5952

Mark Snell, Chief Deputy Secretary of State and Chief of Staff
Lucas Building, 1st Floor
321 East 12th Street
Des Moines, Iowa 50319
515/242-5083   FAX 515/281-4682

Michael Ross, Deputy Secretary of State
515/725-2874   FAX 515/281-4682

Carol Olson, Deputy Secretary of State for Elections
515/281-0145   FAX 515/281-4682
1-888/767-8683 (Toll Free)

Dawn Williams, Director of Elections
515/281-0145   FAX 515/281-4682

Business Services
515/281-5204   FAX 515/242-5953

-Candidates on Ballot
-Election Results
-Constitutional Amendments
-Voting Systems Certification
-Voter Registration
-Voting Accessibility
-Corporate Registration

ETHICS AND CAMPAIGN DISCLOSURE BOARD

Megan Tooker, Executive Director and Counsel
Ethics and Campaign Disclosure Board
510 East 12th Street, Suite 1A
Des Moines, Iowa 50319
URL http://www.iowa.gov/ethics
E-Mail: megan.tooker@iowa.gov
515/281-4028   FAX 515/281-4073

> Jason Hacker, Statewide PAC and County Party Auditor
> *E-Mail: jason.hacker@iowa.gov*
> Cohl Bultje, Statewide Candidate and Party Auditor
> *E-Mail: cohl.bultje@iowa.gov*
> Sharon Wright, Administrative Assistant
> *E-Mail: sharon.wright@iowa.gov*
> Tim Annee, County/Local Candidate and PAC Auditor
> *E-Mail: tim.annee@iowa.gov*
> Vanessa Sayasane, Legislative Candidate Auditor
> *E-Mail: Vanessa.Sayasane2@iowa.gov*

-Federal Campaign Finance Reports
    (Online via FEC.gov)
-Federal Personal Financial Reports
-State Campaign Finance Reports
-County and Local Campaign Finance Reports
-Executive Branch Lobbyists' and Clients' Reports
-Executive Branch Personal Finance Reports
-Executive Branch Ethics/Conflicts of Interest
-Income Tax Checkoff Reports
-State Party Building Fund Reports
-Agency Gifts and Bequests Reports

TREASURER OF STATE

Michael L. Fitzgerald (Elected, D)
Treasurer of State
Capitol Building, Room 114
Des Moines, Iowa 50319
URL http://www.iowatreasurer.gov
E-Mail: treasurer@iowa.gov
515/281-5368 FAX 515/281-7562

Karen Austin, Deputy Treasurer
321 East 12th Street, 1st Floor
Des Moines, Iowa 50319
E-Mail: Karen.austin@iowa.gov
515/281-7677

Stephanie Devin, Deputy Treasurer
321 East 12th Street, 1st Floor
Des Moines, Iowa 50319
E-Mail: Stefanie.devin@iowa.gov
515/281-5957

*
* -Maintenance of Public Financing Funds
* -Trustee of IPERS, PORS and the Judicial
*   Retirement Fund
* -Issues Annual Report of Bonded Indebtedness
*   of State and Local Governments In Iowa

DEPARTMENT OF REVENUE

Courtney M. Kay-Decker, Director
Department of Revenue
Hoover State Office Building, 4th Floor
1305 East Walnut Street
Des Moines, Iowa 50319
URL https://tax.iowa.gov
E-Mail: Courtney.Decker@iowa.gov
515/281-3204 FAX 515/242-6156

Information/Taxpayer Services
515/281-3114

* -Collection of Public Financing Funds and
*   Disbursement

STATE LEGISLATURE

Michael E. Marshall, Secretary of the Senate
State Capitol
Des Moines, Iowa 50319
E-Mail: mike.marshall@legis.iowa.gov
515/281-5307 FAX 515/242-6108

   Kathy Stachon, Senate Lobbyist Clerk
   E-Mail: kathy.stachon@legis.iowa.gov
   515/281-5932

Carmine Boal, Chief Clerk of the House
State Capitol
Des Moines, Iowa 50319
E-Mail: carmine.boal@legis.iowa.gov
515/281-4280 FAX 581/281-8758

* -Lobby Reports
* -Lobby Client Reports
* -Session Function Registrations
* -Session Function Reports
* -Senate Personal Financial Disclosures

* -Lobby Reports
* -Lobby Client Reports
* -Session Function Registrations
* -Session Function Reports
* -House Personal Financial Disclosures

LEGISLATIVE REFERENCE

Glen Dickinson, Director	* -Legislative Bills and Amendments
Legislative Services Agency	
State Capitol, G01	
Des Moines, Iowa 50319	
URL http://www.legis.iowa.gov	
E-Mail: glen.dickinson@legis.iowa.gov	
515/281-3566 FAX 515/281-8027	

Richard Johnson, Legal Services Division Director
E-Mail: richard.johnson@legis.iowa.gov
Ed Cook, Senior Legal Counsel
E-Mail: ed.cook@legis.iowa.gov
Susan E. Crowley, Legal Editor
E-Mail: susan.crowley@legis.iowa.gov

ATTORNEY GENERAL

Thomas Miller (Elected, D)   -Other Court Actions
Attorney General of Iowa
1305 East Walnut Street
Des Moines, Iowa 50319
URL http://www.iowaattorneygeneral.gov
515/281-5164 FAX 515/281-4209

KANSAS

SECRETARY OF STATE

Kris W. Kobach (Elected, R)
Secretary of State
Memorial Hall, 1st Floor
120 S.W. 10th Avenue
Topeka, Kansas 66612-1594
URL http://www.sos.ks.gov
785/296-4564 FAX 785/368-8033

    Bryan Caskey, Deputy Assistant Secretary of State
       for Elections/Legislative Matters
    E-Mail: bryan.caskey@sos.ks.gov
    785/296-4561 FAX 785/291-3051

    Craig McCullah, Public Affairs Director
    Jameson Beckner, HAVA Coordinator

Kathy Sachs, Deputy Assistant Secretary of State
Business Services Division
E-Mail: kathy.sachs@sos.ks.gov
785/296-4564 FAX 785/296-4570

-Candidates on Ballot
-Election Results
-Federal Campaign Finance Reports
    (Online via FEC.gov)
-Federal Personal Financial Reports
-State Campaign Finance Reports
-State Personal Financial Reports
-State Lobby Reports
-Voting Accessibility

-Corporate Registration

GOVERNMENTAL ETHICS COMMISSION

Carol E. Williams, Executive Director
Governmental Ethics Commission
901 South Kansas Avenue
Topeka, Kansas 66612-1287
URL http://www.kansas.gov/ethics
E-Mail: cewms@ethics.ks.gov and *ethics@ ethics.ks.gov*
785/296-4219 FAX 785/296-2548

    Bill Beightel, Investigator
    Brett Berry, Attorney
    Rita Phannenstiel, Lobbyist Coordinator
    Karina Renna, State Campaign Finance Supervisor
    Jen Schneider, Local Campaign Finance Supervisor
    Roxie Valdivia, Auditor
    Jessica White, Auditor

-Reviews Disclosure Reports for Compliance with
    Campaign, Ethics and Lobby Laws
-Administers and Enforces the State's Campaign
    Finance, Lobbying and Conflict of Interest
    Laws

LEGISLATIVE REFERENCE

Joanne Budler, State Librarian
State Library of Kansas
300 S.W. 10th Avenue, Room 312-N
Topeka, Kansas 66612-1593
URL http://kslib.info/Ask (Text and Chat Services Available)
785/296-3296 FAX (Supplied Upon Request)
1-800/432-3924 (Toll Free in State)

    Legislative Reference
    E-Mail: infodesk@ks.gov
    785/296-2149

-Bill Status
-General Reference/Statutory Information
-Government Policy
-Legislative History
-State and Federal Documents
-Statewide Library Resources

ATTORNEY GENERAL

Derek Schmidt (Elected, R)
Attorney General of Kansas
Memorial Hall, 2nd Floor
120 S.W. 10th Avenue
Topeka, Kansas 66612-1597
URL http://www.ag.ks.gov
E-Mail: general@ksag.org
785/296-2215   FAX 785/296-6296
TTY 1-800/766-3777

*
*   -Other Court Actions
*
*
*
*
*
*
*

KENTUCKY

SECRETARY OF STATE

Alison Lundergan Grimes (Elected, D)
Secretary of State
Chair of State Board of Elections
State Capitol, Suite 152
700 Capitol Avenue
Frankfort, Kentucky 40601-3493
URL http://www.sos.ky.gov
E-Mail: sos.secretary@ky.gov
502/564-3490   FAX 502/564-5687

    Lindsay Hughes Thurston, Assistant Secretary of State
    E-Mail: lindsay.thurston@ky.gov
    502/782-7417
    Mary Sue Helm, Director of Elections
    E-Mail: marysue.helm@ky.gov
    502/782-7416

-Candidates on Ballot
-Corporate Registration/Business Filings

REGISTRY OF ELECTION FINANCE

John R. Steffen, Executive Director
Kentucky Registry of Election Finance
140 Walnut Street
Frankfort, Kentucky 40601-3240
URL http://www.kref.ky.gov
E-Mail: john.steffen@ky.gov
502/573-2226   FAX 502/573-5622

    Emily Dennis, General Counsel
    E-Mail: emily.dennis@ky.gov

-Federal Campaign Finance Reports
    (Online via FEC.gov)
-Federal Personal Financial Reports
-State Campaign Finance Reports
-State Financial Disclosure Reports
    (Commonwealth Attorneys and Judges)
-Ballot Issues Spending Reports
-Advisory Opinions
-Electronic Filings

STATE BOARD OF ELECTIONS

Maryellen Allen, Executive Director
State Board of Elections
140 Walnut Street
Frankfort, Kentucky 40601-3240
URL http://www.elect.ky.gov
E-Mail: maryellen.allen@ky.gov
502/573-7100   FAX 502/573-4369

    Matthew Selph, Assistant Director
    E-Mail: matthew.selph@ky.gov

-Statewide Voter Registration Database
-Election Results
-Voting Irregularities Reports from Counties
-Voting Accessibility
-Supervise Conduct of Elections
-Compliance Officer for all State and Federal
    Election Laws

EXECUTIVE BRANCH ETHICS COMMISSION

Kathryn H. Gabhart, Executive Director
Executive Branch Ethics Commission
#3 Fountain Place
Frankfort, Kentucky 40601
URL http://ethics.ky.gov
E-Mail: katie.gabhart@ky.gov
502/564-7954   FAX 502/564-2686

-Executive Branch Personal Financial Disclosure
    Reports
-Executive Agency Lobbyists' Registration and
    Reports
-Advisory Opinions

LEGISLATIVE ETHICS COMMISSION

H. John Schaaf, Executive Director
Legislative Ethics Commission
22 Mill Creek Park
Frankfort, Kentucky 40601
URL http://klec.ky.gov
502/573-2863 FAX 502/573-2929

    Donnita Crittenden, Principal Assistant
    E-Mail: donnita.crittenden@lrc.ky.gov
    Kara Daniel, Legal Counsel
    E-Mail: kara.daniel@lrc.ky.gov

-Advisory Opinions
-State Personal Financial Reports
    (Legislative Branch)
-State Lobby Reports

STATE TREASURER

Allison Ball (Elected, R)
State Treasurer
1050 US Highway 127 South, Suite 100
Frankfort, Kentucky 40601
URL http://www.kytreasury.com
502/564-4722 FAX 502/564-6545
1-800/465-4722

-Disbursement of Public Financing Funds to
    Political Parties from Tax Check-offs Based
    on Calculations Prepared by State
    Finance Cabinet

FINANCE AND ADMINISTRATION CABINET

Daniel P. Bork, Commissioner
Kentucky Department of Revenue
State Office Building
501 High Street
Frankfort, Kentucky 40620
URL http://finance.ky.gov
502/564-3226 FAX 502/564-3875

-Collection and Certification of Public Financing
    Funds to Political Parties from Tax Check-offs

LEGISLATIVE RESEARCH COMMISSION

David Byerman, Director
Legislative Research Commission
State Capitol, Room 300
700 Capitol Avenue
Frankfort, Kentucky 40601
URL http://www.lrc.ky.gov
502/564-8100 FAX 502/564-2922

-State Legislative Information, Including Introduced
    Legislation
-State Statutes and Regulations

ATTORNEY GENERAL

Andy Beshear (Elected, D)
Attorney General of Kentucky
700 Capitol Avenue
State Capitol, Suite 118
Frankfort, Kentucky 40601-3449
URL http://www.ag.ky.gov
E-Mail: attorney.general@ag.ky.gov
502/696-5300   FAX 502/564-2894

OAG Election Fraud Hotline
1-800/328-8683

*
*   -Investigates and Prosecutes Election Law,
*   Including Violations of Campaign Finance
*   Law
*   -Investigates and Prosecutes Public Corruption
*   -Registration of Professional Solicitors Conducting
*   Active Charitable Campaigns
*   -Open Records and Open Meetings
*   -Business Filings
*
*
*

SECRETARY OF STATE

Tom Schedler (Elected, R)
Secretary of State
8585 Archives Avenue
Baton Rouge, Louisiana 70809
URL http://www.sos.la.gov
225/922-2880   FAX 225/922-2003
    Mailing Address:
    P.O. Box 94125
    Baton Rouge, Louisiana 70804-9125

    Merietta Norton, General Counsel
    8585 Archives Avenue
    Baton Rouge, Louisiana 70809
    225/287-7477   FAX 225/922-1180

Angie Rogers
Commissioner of Elections
8585 Archives Avenue
Baton Rouge, Louisiana 70809
E-Mail: angie.rogers@sos.la.gov
225/922-0900   FAX 225/922-0945
    Mailing Address:
    P.O. Box 94125
    Baton Rouge, Louisiana 70804-9125

Erin Delany, Director of Elections
Balloting, Publications and Commissions
8585 Archives Avenue
Baton Rouge, Louisiana 70809
E-Mail: elections@sos.la.gov
225/922-0900   FAX 225/922-0945
    Mailing Address:
    P.O. Box 94125
    Baton Rouge, Louisiana 70804-9125

    Heather Meyers
    Teri Reine
    Stephanie Sasser

Joanne Reed, Director of Registration
8585 Archives Avenue
Baton Rouge, Louisiana 70809
E-Mail: elections@sos.la.gov
225/922-0900   FAX 225/922-1167
    Mailing Address:
    P.O. Box 94125
    Baton Rouge, Louisiana 70804-9125

-Candidates on Ballot
-Election Results
-Federal Campaign Finance Reports
    (Online via FEC.gov)
-Federal Personal Financial Reports
-Printing, Storage and Shipping of all
    Election Supplies
-Voting Accessibility
-Voter Registration
-Voting Machines and Absentee Counting
    Equipment
-Chief Election Officer for NVRA
-HAVA Implementation

(Continued on Next Page)

SECRETARY OF STATE (Continued)

Sherri Hadskey, Director of Field Operations
8585 Archives Avenue
Baton Rouge, Louisiana 70809
E-Mail: elections@sos.la.gov
225/922-2486 FAX 225/922-0826
    Mailing Address:
    P.O. Box 94125
    Baton Rouge, Louisiana 70804-9125

    Shanie Bourg
    Jason Caillouet
    Kevin Paul
    Mike West

Carla Bonaventure, Commercial Division Administrator   -Corporate Registration
8585 Archives Avenue
Baton Rouge, Louisiana 70809
E-Mail: cbonaventure@sos.la.gov
225/925-4716 FAX 225/932-5320
    Mailing Address:
    P.O. Box 94125
    Baton Rouge, Louisiana 70804-9125

BOARD OF ETHICS AND SUPERVISORY COMMITTEE ON CAMPAIGN FINANCE DISCLOSURE

Kathleen Allen, Ethics Administrator
Board of Ethics
617 North Third Street
LaSalle Building, Suite 10-36
Baton Rouge, Louisiana 70802
URL http://www.ethics.state.la.us
E-Mail: kathleen.allen@la.gov
Phone: 225/219-5600 FAX 225/381-7271
1-800/842-6630 (Toll Free)
    Mailing Address:
    P.O. Box 4368
    Baton Rouge, Louisiana 70821

    Chris Sommers, Director, Campaign Finance and Lobbying
      Division
    Robin Gremillion, Director, Disclosure Division
    Jenny Arnaud, Compliance Officer
    Tracy Barker, Attorney
    Jennifer Land, Attorney
    Suzanne Mooney, Attorney

-State Campaign Finance Reports (Filed at State,
    Parish and Local Levels)
-State Personal Financial Reports (Filed at State,
    Parish and Local Levels)
-State Lobby Registration
-Lobbyists Expenditure Disclosure Reports
-Electronic Filings
-Local Lobby Registration

LEGISLATIVE REFERENCE

Frances Thomas, Director
David R. Poynter Legislative Research Library
P.O. Box 94012
Baton Rouge, Louisiana 70804-9012
URL http://house.legis.state.la.us (House of Representatives Page)
225/342-2430 FAX 225/342-2431

(Continued on Next Page)

LEGISLATIVE REFERENCE (Continued)

Bryan Vincent, Director
Governmental Affairs Division
House Legislative Services
Louisiana House of Representatives
P.O. Box 44486
Baton Rouge, Louisiana 70804
225/342-2398 FAX 225/342-2392

Patricia Lowrey-Dufour   -Legislation concerning Ethics and Elections for the
House Legislative Services   House of Representatives
Louisiana House of Representatives
P.O. Box 44486
Baton Rouge, Louisiana 70804
E-Mail: lowreyp@legis.la.gov
225/342-2396 FAX 225/377-2310

Mark Mahaffey
House Legislative Services
Louisiana House of Representatives
P.O. Box 44486
Baton Rouge, Louisiana 70804
E-Mail: mahaffem@legis.la.gov
225/342-2598 FAX 225/376-5966

STATE LEGISLATURE

Glenn Koepp, Secretary of the Senate   -Senators' Income Disclosure Reports
P.O. Box 94183   -Redistricting Plans
Baton Rouge, Louisiana 70804
URL http://senate.la.gov/secretary/
E-Mail: koeppg@legis.la.gov
225/342-5997 FAX 225/342-1140

Alfred W. Speer, Clerk of the House   -Redistricting Plans
P.O. Box 44281
Baton Rouge, Louisiana 70804
URL http://house.louisiana.gov/H_Staff/H_Staff_ClerksOffice.asp
E-Mail: speera@legis.la.gov
225/342-7259 FAX 225/342-5045

ATTORNEY GENERAL

Jeff Landry (Elected, R)   -Other Court Actions
Attorney General of Louisiana
1885 North 3rd Street
Baton Rouge, Louisiana 70802
URL http://www.ag.state.la.us
225/326-6079 FAX 225/326-6797
    Mailing Address:
    P.O. Box 94005
    Baton Rouge, Louisiana 70804-9005

    Wilbur "Bill" Stiles, Chief Deputy Attorney General
    225/326-6705 FAX 225/326-6797

SECRETARY OF STATE

Matthew Dunlap (Elected by Legislature, D)	*
Secretary of State	*
148 State House Station	*
Augusta, Maine 04333-0148	*
URL http://www.maine.gov/sos	*
207/626-8400 FAX 207/287-8598	*

Julie L. Flynn, Deputy Secretary of State
Bureau of Corporations, Elections and Commissions
101 State House Station
Augusta, Maine 04333-0101
207/624-7736 FAX 207/287-5874

    Melissa Packard, Director of Elections and Administrative   -Candidates on Ballot
        Procedure Act   -Election Results
       E-Mail: melissa.packard@maine.gov   -Voting Accessibility
       207/624-7650 FAX 207/287-6545

    Tracy Willett, Assistant Director of Elections

Division of Corporations   -Corporate Registration
207/624-7752 FAX 207/287-5874

COMMISSION ON GOVERNMENTAL ETHICS AND ELECTION PRACTICES

Jonathan Wayne, Executive Director   -Federal Campaign Finance Reports
Commission on Governmental Ethics and Election Practices   (Online via FEC.gov)
135 State House Station   -Federal Personal Financial Reports
Augusta, Maine 04333   -State Campaign Finance Reports
URL http://www.maine.gov/ethics   -State Personal Financial Reports
E-Mail: jonathan.wayne@maine.gov   -State Initiative/Referendum Spending Reports
207/287-4179 FAX 207/287-6775   -State Lobby Reports

    Paul Lavin, Assistant Director
    Lorrie Brann, Commission Assistant
    Emma Burke, Candidate Registrar
    Erin Gordon, Candidate Registrar
    Benjamin Dyer, Political Committee and Lobbyist Registrar

MAINE REVENUE SERVICES

Jerome D. Gerard, Executive Director   -Collection of Public Financing Funds
Maine Revenue Services
P.O. Box 1060
Augusta, Maine 04332-1060
URL http://www.maine.gov/revenue
207/624-9677 FAX 207/287-3618

LEGISLATIVE REFERENCE

	*
John R. Barden, Director	*
Law and Legislative Reference Library	*
43 State House Station	*
Augusta, Maine 04333-0043	*
URL http://legislature.maine.gov/lawlibrary	*
207/287-1600 FAX 207/287-6467	*
TTY 207/287-6431	*

ATTORNEY GENERAL

	*	
	*	
Janet T. Mills (Elected by Legislature, D)	*	-Other Court Actions
Attorney General of Maine	*	
6 State House Station	*	
Augusta, Maine 04333	*	
URL http://www.maine.gov/ag	*	
207/626-8800 FAX 207/287-3145	*	
TTY 207/626-8865	*	

SECRETARY OF STATE

John C. Wobensmith (Appointed, R)
Secretary of State
16 Francis Street
Annapolis, Maryland 21401
URL http://www.sos.state.md.us
E-Mail: dlmdsos_sos@maryland.gov
410/974-5521 FAX 410/974-5190
1-888/874-0013
TDD 410/333-3098

-Candidates on Ballot (Presidential Primary)
-Ballot Captions for Voter Referendums and
   Constitutional Amendments
-Petitions for Referendum
-Member of the State Board of Canvassers

STATE BOARD OF ELECTIONS

Linda Lamone, Administrator
State Board of Elections
151 West Street, Suite 200
Annapolis, Maryland 21401
URL http://www.elections.maryland.gov
E-Mail: info.sbe@maryland.gov
410/269-2840 FAX 410/974-2019
1-800/222-8683 (Toll Free)
   Mailing Address:
   P.O. Box 6486
   Annapolis, Maryland 21401-0486

   Nikki Charlson, Deputy State Administrator
   Jared DeMarinis, Director, Candidacy and Campaign Finance
   Donna J. Duncan, Assistant Deputy for Election Management
   Erin Perrone, Election Reform Director
   Mary Cramer Wagner, Director, Voter Registration Division

-Candidates on Ballot
-Ballot Questions
-Election Results
-Federal Campaign Finance Reports
   (Online via FEC.gov)
-Federal Personal Financial Reports
-State Campaign Finance Reports (Online)
-Reports on Allocation and Authorization of Public
   Financing Funds
-Reports of Contributions to State Candidates by
   Corporations Doing Business with the State
-Administration of Fair Campaign Practicing Act
-Electronic Filings
-Voting Accessibility
-Businesses which Receive Disclosure Statements
   Of $100,000 or More in State Contracts

STATE ETHICS COMMISSION

Michael W. Lord, Executive Director
State Ethics Commission
45 Calvert Street, 3rd Floor
Annapolis, Maryland 21401
URL http://ethics.maryland.gov/
410/260-7770 FAX 410/260-7747
1-877-669-6085 (Toll Free)

Jennifer K. Allgair, General Counsel, General Inquiries, Advisory
   Opinions, Local Government
Katherine Thompson, Assistant General Counsel
William J. Colquhoun, Staff Counsel, Enforcement Matters

-State Lobbying Registration and Activity Reports
-Annual Financial Disclosure Statements for State
   and Elected Officials
-Board and Commission Member Time of
   Appointment Exemption Forms
-Published Advisory Opinions
-Lists of Entities Doing Business with the State
-Ethics Enforcement Case Decisions
-Guidance and Approval of Local Government
   Ethics Laws
-Standards for Conduct for all State
   Employees and Regulated Lobbyists
-Training for Public Officials and Regulated and
   Potential Lobbyists

JOINT COMMITTEE ON LEGISLATIVE ETHICS

Deadra W. Daly, Ethics Counsel
Department of Legislative Services
90 State Circle
Annapolis, Maryland 21401-1991
URL http://dls.state.md.us
410/946-5200 FAX 410/946-5205

-Ethics Disclosure by the Members of the Maryland
   General Assembly
-Ethics Enforcement over Members
-Ethics Opinions

LEGISLATIVE SERVICES

Karl Aro, Executive Director
Department of Legislative Services
90 State Circle
Annapolis, Maryland 21401-1991
URL http://dls.state.md.us
E-Mail: mgaleg@maryland.gov
410/946-5400   FAX 410/946-5205

* -Drafting Legislation and Amendments
* -Research and Legal Review
* -Statutory Revisions
* -Committee Staffing
* -Budget Analysis
* -Program Evaluation
* -Audits

STATE DEPARTMENT OF ASSESSMENTS AND TAXATION

Corporate Charter Division
301 West Preston Street, Room 801
Baltimore, Maryland 21201-2395
URL http://dat.maryland.gov
E-Mail: charterhelp@maryland.gov
410/767-1340
1-888/246-5941 (Toll Free in State)

* -Corporate Registration

COMPTROLLER OF MARYLAND

Peter Franchot (Elected, D)
Comptroller of Maryland
P.O. Box 466
Annapolis, Maryland 21404-0466
URL http://www.marylandtaxes.com
E-Mail: pfranchot@comp.state.md.us
410/260-7801   FAX 410/974-3808

* -Member of the State Board of Canvassers
* -Disbursement of Public Financing Funds
* -Administers Contribution Provision on Maryland
    Income Tax Returns

ATTORNEY GENERAL

Brian E. Frosh (Elected, D)
Attorney General of Maryland
200 Saint Paul Place
Baltimore, Maryland 21202
URL http://www.oag.state.md.us
E-Mail: oag@oag.state.md.us
410/576-6300   FAX 410/576-7036
1-888/743-0023 (Toll Free)

* -Member of the State Board of Canvassers
* -Other Court Actions

SECRETARY OF THE COMMONWEALTH

William F. Galvin (Elected, D)
Secretary of the Commonwealth
State House, Room 337
Boston, Massachusetts 02133
URL http://www.sec.state.ma.us
617/727-9180 FAX 617/742-4722

Elections Division
McCormack Building, Room 1705
One Ashburton Place
Boston, Massachusetts 02108
E-Mail: elections@sec.state.ma.us
617/727-2828 FAX 617/742-3238
1-800/462-8683 (Toll Free in State)

-Candidates on Ballot
-Election Results
-Voting Accessibility

    Michelle K. Tassinari, Director and Legal Counsel
    Rebecca S. Murray, Assistant Director and Associate Legal
       Counsel
    William Rosenberry, Election Services Manager
    Harry J. Petrucci, Field Representative
    Calvin T. Brown, Election Specialist
    Michael D'Argenio, Election Specialist
    Howard Hock, Election Specialist
    James McGowan, Election Specialist
    Bridget Simmons Murphy, Election Specialist
    Debra O'Malley, Election Specialist

Lobbyist Division
McCormack Building, Room 1719
One Ashburton Place
Boston, Massachusetts 02108
E-mail: lob@sec.state.ma.us
617/727-9122 FAX 617/727-5914

-Federal Campaign Finance Reports
   (Online via FEC.gov)
-Federal Personal Financial Reports
-State Lobbyist Reports

    Marie D. Marra, Director
    Ivana Licakova, Clerk

Laurie Flynn, Chief Legal Counsel, Director of Corporations
McCormack Building, Room 1713
One Ashburton Place
Boston, Massachusetts 02108
E-Mail: corpinfo@sec.state.ma.us
617/727-4919 FAX 617/878-3505

-Corporate Registration

OFFICE OF CAMPAIGN AND POLITICAL FINANCE

Michael J. Sullivan, Director
Office of Campaign and Political Finance
One Ashburton Place, Room 411
Boston, Massachusetts 02108
URL http://www.ocpf.us
E-Mail: OCPF@cpf.state.ma.us
617/979-8300 FAX 617/727-6549
1-800/462-6273 (Toll Free in State)

    Gregory H. Birne, General Counsel
    Jason Tait, Director of Public Information
    Patricia Jacobson, Director of Auditing

-Campaign Finance Reports for State and County
    Candidates, PAC's, Political Party Committees,
    Mayoral, City Council and Alderman
    Candidates In Cities with Populations of
    75,000 or More, and All Other Mayoral
    Candidates.
-State Initiative/Referendum Spending
-State Public Financing Documentation
-Administration of Public Financing System
-Oversight of Public Employees' Campaign Finance
    Activity at State, County and Municipal Levels

STATE ETHICS COMMISSION

Karen L. Nober, Executive Director
Massachusetts State Ethics Commission
One Ashburton Place, Room 619
Boston, Massachusetts 02108
URL http://www.mass.gov/ethics
617/371-9500 FAX 617/723-5851
1-888/485-4766 (Toll Free in State)

    Deirdre Roney, General Counsel & Chief, Legal Division
    Kelly A. Downes, Chief, Enforcement Division
    David Giannotti, Chief, Communications & Public Education
        Division

-State Personal Financial Disclosure Reports
-Enforcement and Interpretation of Massachusetts
    Conflict of Interest and Financial Disclosure
    Laws for all State, Municipal and
    County Employees

COMPTROLLER

Thomas G. Shack III, Esq. (Appointed)
Comptroller
One Ashburton Place, 9th Floor
Boston, Massachusetts 02108
URL http://www.mass.gov/ctr
E-Mail: comptroller.info@state.ma.us
617/727-5000

    Jeffrey Shapiro, Esq., Deputy Comptroller and Chief Operating
        Officer
    Howard Merkowitz, Deputy Comptroller
    Christopher Guido, Deputy Comptroller
    Kathy Sheppard, Deputy Comptroller
    Jenny Hedderman, Deputy Comptroller and General Counsel

-Certifies Size of Public Financing Funds
-Publishes Official Financial Reports
-Oversight and Enforcement of State Finance Laws

TREASURER OF THE COMMONWEALTH

Deborah B. Goldberg (Elected, D)
Treasurer and Receiver General of the Commonwealth
State House, Room 227
Boston, Massachusetts 02133
URL http://www.mass.gov/treasury/
617/367-6900 FAX 617/248-6900

-Collection of Public Financing Funds
-Collection and Investment of Public Funds

LEGISLATIVE REFERENCE

William F. Welch, Clerk of the Senate
State House, Room 335
Boston, Massachusetts 02133
E-Mail: william.f.welch@masenate.gov
617/722-1276

Steven T. James, Clerk of the House
State House, Room 145
Boston, Massachusetts 02133
URL http://malegislature.gov/
E-Mail: steven.james@mahouse.gov
617/722-2356

ATTORNEY GENERAL

Maura Healey (Elected, D)
Attorney General of Massachusetts
One Ashburton Place, 20th Floor
Boston, Massachusetts 02108-1698
URL http://www.mass.gov/ago
617/727-2200   FAX 617/727-3251

-Other Court Actions

MICHIGAN

SECRETARY OF STATE

Ruth Johnson (Elected, R)
Secretary of State
430 West Allegan Street, 4th Floor
Lansing, Michigan 48918-1700
URL http://www.michigan.gov/sos
517/373-2510 FAX 517/373-0727

Christopher M. Thomas, Director of Elections
430 West Allegan Street, 1st Floor
Lansing, Michigan 48918-1700
E-Mail: christopherT@michigan.gov
517/373-2540 FAX 517/373-0941
    Mailing Address:
    P.O. Box 20126
    Lansing, Michigan 48901-0726

    Evelyn Quiroga, Director, Disclosure Data Division
    E-Mail: quirogae1@michigan.gov
    Timothy M. Hanson, Director, Program Development Division
    E-Mail: hansont@michigan.gov
    Sally Williams, Director, Elections Liaison Division
    E-Mail: williamsS1@michigan.gov

-Candidates on Ballot
-Election Results
-Federal Campaign Finance Reports
    (Online via FEC.gov)
-Federal Personal Financial Reports
-State Campaign Finance Reports
-State Lobby Reports
-State Initiative/Referendum Spending Reports
-State Public Financing Documentation
-Certification of Amounts of Public Financing
-Electronic Filings
-Qualified Voter File (Voter Registration
    Information)

MICHIGAN STATE BOARD OF ETHICS

John Gnodtke, Executive Secretary
Michigan State Board of Ethics
400 South Pine Street
P.O. Box 30002
Lansing, Michigan 48909
E-Mail: ethicsboard@michigan.gov
517/373-3644 FAX 517/373-3103

-Investigations of Ethical Conduct of State Public
    Officers and Employees
-Advisory Opinions

STATE TREASURER

Nick A. Khouri (Appointed, R)
State Treasurer
Michigan Department of Treasury
430 W. Allegan Street
Lansing, Michigan 48922
URL http://www.michigan.gov/treasury
517/373-3223 FAX 517/335-1785

-Collection, Maintenance and Distribution of Public
    Financing Funds
-Investment of Public Pension Funds

LEGISLATIVE REFERENCE

John C. Bollman, Interim Legislative Council Administrator
Legislative Service Bureau
124 West Allegan Street, 3rd Floor
P.O. Box 30036
Lansing, Michigan 48933
URL http://www.legislature.mi.gov
517/373-0212 FAX: 517/373-7668

DEPARTMENT OF LICENSING AND REGULATORY AFFAIRS

James Lotoszinski, Director
Corporations Division
Corporations, Securities and Commercial Licensing Bureau
P.O. Box 30054
Lansing, Michigan 48909-0538
URL http://www.michigan.gov/corporations
E-Mail: corpsmail@michigan.gov
517/241-6470   FAX 517/241-0538

-Corporate Registration

ATTORNEY GENERAL

Bill Schuette (Elected, R)
Attorney General of Michigan
G. Mennen Williams Building, 7th Floor
525 West Ottawa Street
P.O. Box 30212
Lansing, Michigan 48909
URL http://www.michigan.gov/ag
517/373-1110   FAX 517/373-3042

-Issues Opinions Binding on State Officers and
    Agencies Regarding Questions on Conflicts
    of Interest and Incompatible Offices
-Other Court Actions

MINNESOTA

SECRETARY OF STATE

Steve Simon (Elected, DFL)
Secretary of State
180 State Office Building
100 Rev. Dr. Martin Luther King, Jr. Boulevard
St. Paul, Minnesota 55155-1299
URL http://www.sos.state.mn.us
E-Mail: secretary.state@state.mn.us
651/201-1324   FAX 651/296-9073

    Ann Kaner-Roth, Deputy Secretary of State
    E-Mail: ann.kaner-roth@state.mn.us

Gary Poser, Director of Elections
Election Division
E-Mail: gary.poser@state.mn.us
651/215-1440   FAX 651/296-9073
1-877-600-8683 (Toll Free)

- Candidates on Ballot
- Election Results
- Federal Campaign Finance Reports
  (Online via FEC.gov)
- Federal Personal Financial Reports
- Voting Accessibility
- Maps

Business Services Division
60 Empire Drive, Suite 100
Saint Paul, Minnesota 55103
E-Mail: business.services@state.mn.us
651/296-2803   FAX 651/297-7067
1-877-551-6767 (Toll Free)

- Corporate Registration

CAMPAIGN FINANCE AND PUBLIC DISCLOSURE BOARD

Gary Goldsmith, Executive Director
Minnesota Campaign Finance and Public Disclosure Board
658 Cedar Street, Suite 190
St. Paul, Minnesota 55155-1603
URL http://www.cfboard.state.mn.us
E-Mail: gary.goldsmith@state.mn.us
651/539-1190   FAX 651/539-1196
1-800/657-3889 (Toll Free)   1-800/357-4114 (Toll Free FAX)

- State Campaign Finance Reports
- State Personal Financial Reports
- State Lobby Reports
- State Public Financing Allocation and Verification
- Electronic Filings
- Disbursement of Public Funds to Candidates

    Jeff Sigurdson, Assistant Director
    E-Mail: jeff.sigurdson@state.mn.us

DEPARTMENT OF REVENUE

Cynthia Bauerly, Commissioner
Department of Revenue
600 North Robert Street
Mail Station 7100
St. Paul, Minnesota 55146-7100
URL http://www.revenue.state.mn.us
E-Mail: cynthia.bauerly@state.mn.us
651/556-6003   FAX 651/556-3133

- Certification of Amounts of Public Financing
  Funds to Candidates

LEGISLATIVE REFERENCE

Elizabeth Lincoln, Director
Legislative Reference Library
645 State Office Building
100 Rev. Dr. Martin Luther King, Jr. Boulevard
St. Paul, Minnesota 55155
URL http://www.leg.mn/lrl
E-Mail: elincoln@lrl.leg.mn
651/296-8338   FAX 651/296-9731

Michele L. Timmons, Revisor
Revisor of Statutes Office
700 State Office Building
100 Rev. Dr. Martin Luther King, Jr. Boulevard
St. Paul, Minnesota 55155-1297
URL http://www.revisor.mn.gov
E-Mail: revisor@revisor.mn.gov
651/296-2868   FAX 651/296-0569

ATTORNEY GENERAL

Lori Swanson (Elected, DFL)
Attorney General of Minnesota
1400 Bremer Tower
445 Minnesota Street
St. Paul, Minnesota 55101
URL http://www.ag.state.mn.us
E-Mail: attorney.general@ag.state.mn.us
651/296-3353   FAX 651/297-4193
1-800/657-3787 (Toll Free)
TTY 651/297-7206 and 1-800/366-4812

-Other Court Actions

SECRETARY OF STATE

Delbert Hosemann (Elected, R)
Secretary of State
401 Mississippi Street
Jackson, Mississippi 39201
URL http://www.sos.ms.gov
601/359-1350 FAX 601/359-1499
1-800/829-6786 (Toll Free)
    Mailing Address:
    P.O. Box 136
    Jackson, Mississippi 39205-0136

    Kimberly P. Turner, Assistant Secretary of State
    Elections Division
    E-Mail: kim.turner@sos.ms.gov
    601/359-5137 FAX 601/576-2545

* -Candidates on Ballot
* -Election Results
* -Federal Campaign Finance Reports
*   (Online via FEC.gov)
* -State Campaign Finance Reports
* -State Lobby Reports
* -Voting Accessibility
* -State Initiatives and Referenda

Thomas H. Riley, III, Assistant Secretary of State
Business Services Division
125 South Congress Street
Jackson, Mississippi 39201
E-Mail: tom.riley@sos.ms.gov
601/359-1633 FAX 601/359-1499

* -Corporate Registration

ETHICS COMMISSION

Tom Hood, Executive Director
Mississippi Ethics Commission
660 North Street, Suite 100-C
Jackson, Mississippi 39202
URL http://www.ethics.state.ms.us
E-Mail: info@ethics.state.ms.us
601/359-1285 FAX 601/359-1292
    Mailing Address:
    P.O. Box 22746
    Jackson, Mississippi 39225-2746

* -State Personal Financial Reports
* -Ethics Laws Administration
* -Open Meeting and Complaints
* -Public Records Opinions

LEGISLATIVE REFERENCE

Senate Docket Office
P.O. Box 1018
Jackson, Mississippi 39215-1018
URL http://www.legislature.ms.gov (Legislature Page)
601/359-3229 FAX 601/359-3935

Senate Legislative Services
P.O. Box 1018
Jackson, Missisippi 39215-1018
601/359-3217 FAX 601/359-2775

House Docket Office
P.O. Box 1018
Jackson, Mississippi 39215-1018
URL http:// www.legislature.ms.gov (Legislature Page)
601/359-3360 FAX 601/359-3728

(Continued on Next Page)

LEGISLATIVE REFERENCE (Continued)

House Legislative Services
P.O. Box 1018
Jackson, Mississippi, 39215-1018
601/359-3310   FAX 601/359-2928

*
*
*
*
*

ATTORNEY GENERAL

*
Jim Hood (Elected, D)   *   -Other Court Actions
Attorney General of Mississippi   *
Walter Sillers Building, Suite 1200   *
550 High Street   *
P.O. Box 220   *
Jackson, Mississippi 39205-0220   *
URL http://www.ago.state.ms.us   *
E-Mail: msag05@ago.state.ms.us   *
601/359-3680   FAX 601/359-3441   *

SECRETARY OF STATE

Jason Kander (Elected, D)
Secretary of State
State Capitol, Room 208
Jefferson City, Missouri 65101
URL http://www.sos.mo.gov
E-Mail: SOSmain@sos.mo.gov
573/751-4936 FAX 573/522-3082
    Mailing Address:
    P.O. Box 1767
    Jefferson City, Missouri 65102

    Barbara J. Wood, Executive Deputy Secretary of State and
        General Counsel
    John Scott, Chief of Staff

Julie A. Allen
Deputy Chief of Staff (Elections and Information Technology)
600 West Main Street
Jefferson City, Missouri 65101
573/751-2301 FAX 573/526-3242
1-800/669-8683 (Toll Free)
    Mailing Address:
    P.O. Box 1767
    Jefferson City, Missouri 65102

-Candidates on Ballot
-Election Results
-Voting Accessibility

Lesley Lueckenotte, Director of Business Services
600 West Main Street
Jefferson City, Missouri 65101
573/751-4153 FAX 573/751-5841
1-866/223-6535 (Toll Free)
    Mailing Address:
    P.O. Box 778
    Jefferson City, Missouri 65102-0778

-Corporate Registration

MISSOURI ETHICS COMMISSION

James Klahr, Executive Director
Missouri Ethics Commission
3411A Knipp Drive
Jefferson City, Missouri 65109
URL http://www.mec.mo.gov
E-Mail: helpdesk@mec.mo.gov
573/751-2020 FAX 573/526-4506
1-800/392-8660 (Toll Free)
    Mailing Address:
    P.O. Box 1370
    Jefferson City, Missouri 65102

    Stacey Heislen, Deputy Director
    Betsy Byers, Director of Business Services
    Craig Hollis, Director of Information Technology Services
    Elizabeth L. Ziegler, General Counsel

-Federal Campaign Finance Reports
    (Online via FEC.gov)
-Federal Personal Financial Reports
-State Campaign Finance Reports
-State Personal Financial Reports
-State Lobby Reports
-Electronic Filings

LEGISLATIVE RESEARCH

	*
Russ Hembree, Revisor of Statutes	*
Committee on Legislative Research	*
State Capitol, Room 117-A	*
Jefferson City, Missouri 65101	*
URL http://www.moga.mo.gov (General Assembly Page)	*
573/751-4223 FAX 573/751-1476	*

ATTORNEY GENERAL

	*	
Chris Koster (Elected, D)	*	-Other Court Actions
Attorney General of Missouri	*	
Supreme Court Building	*	
207 West High Street	*	
P.O. Box 899	*	
Jefferson City, Missouri 65102	*	
URL http://www.ago.mo.gov	*	
E-Mail: attorney.general@ago.mo.gov	*	
573/751-3321 FAX 573/751-0774	*	

SECRETARY OF STATE

Linda McCulloch (Elected, D)
Secretary of State
State Capitol, Room 260
P.O. Box 202801
Helena, Montana 59620-2801
URL http://www.sos.mt.gov
406/444-2034   FAX 406/444-4249

    Lisa Kimmet, Deputy for Elections   -Candidates on Ballot
    E-Mail: lkimmet@mt.gov   -Election Results
    406/444-5376   FAX 406/444-2023   -Voting Accessibility
    1-888/884-8683 (Toll Free)

Business Services Bureau   -Corporate Registration
E-Mail: business@mt.gov
406/444-3665   FAX 406/444-3976

COMMISSIONER OF POLITICAL PRACTICES

Jonathan Motl   -Federal Campaign Finance Reports
Commissioner of Political Practices   (Online via FEC.gov)
1205 8th Avenue   -Federal Personal Financial Reports
P.O. Box 202401   -State Campaign Finance Reports
Helena, Montana 59620-2401   -State Business Disclosure Financial Reports
URL http://www.politicalpractices.mt.gov   -State Principal Lobbying Financial Reports
E-Mail: jmotl@mt.gov   -State Ballot Issue Committee Financial Reports
406/444-2942   FAX 406/444-1643   -Ethics Laws

LEGISLATIVE REFERENCE

Susan Byorth Fox, Executive Director
Legislative Services Division
State Capitol, Room 110
P.O. Box 201706
Helena, Montana 59620-1706
URL http://www.leg.mt.gov/css/default.asp
E-Mail: sfox@mt.gov
406/444-3064   FAX 406/444-3036

ATTORNEY GENERAL

Tim Fox (Elected, R)   -Other Court Actions
Attorney General of Montana
215 North Sanders, 3rd Floor
P.O. Box 201401
Helena, Montana 59620-1401
URL https://dojmt.gov/
E-Mail: contactdoj@mt.gov
406/444-2026   FAX 406/444-3549

NEBRASKA

SECRETARY OF STATE

John A. Gale (Elected, R)
Secretary of State
State Capitol
1445 K Street, Suite 2300
Lincoln, Nebraska 60508
URL http://www.sos.ne.gov
E-Mail: sos.info@nebraska.gov
402/471-2554 FAX 402/471-3237
    Mailing Address:
    P.O. Box 94608
    Lincoln, Nebraska 68509-4608

Neal Erickson, Director of Elections and Deputy Secretary   -Candidates on Ballot
E-Mail: sos.elect@nebraska.gov   -Election Results
402/471-4127   -Voting Accessibility

Ann Hinkle, Business Services and Technology   -Corporate Registration
402/471-3921

ACCOUNTABILITY AND DISCLOSURE COMMISSION

Frank Daley, Executive Director   -Federal Campaign Finance Reports
Accountability and Disclosure Commission   (Online via FEC.gov)
11th Floor, State Capitol   -Federal Personal Financial Reports
Lincoln, Nebraska 68509   -State Campaign Finance Reports
URL http://nadc.nol.org/   -State Personal Financial Reports
402/471-2522 FAX 402/471-6599   -State Lobby Reports
    Mailing Address: -State Initiative/Referendum Spending Reports
    P.O. Box 95086
    Lincoln, Nebraska 68509-5086

LEGISLATIVE RESEARCH

Nancy Cyr, Director   -Information Regarding Election Laws and
Legislative Research Office   Proposed Legislation
State Capitol, Room 1201   -Legislative Personnel and Process
P.O. Box 94604
Lincoln, Nebraska 68509-4604
URL http://www.nebraskalegislature.gov
E-Mail: ncyr@leg.ne.gov
402/471-2221

ATTORNEY GENERAL

Doug Peterson (Elected, R)   -Public Record/Open Meetings Law Information
Attorney General of Nebraska   -990 Non-Profit Foundation Reports
State Capitol, Room 2115   -Other Court Actions
Lincoln, Nebraska 68509
URL http://www.ago.ne.gov
E-Mail: ago.consumer@nebraska.gov
402/471-2682 FAX 402/471-3297

SECRETARY OF STATE

Barbara Cegavske (Elected, R)
Secretary of State
101 North Carson Street, Suite 3
Carson City, Nevada 89701-4786
URL http://www.nvsos.gov
775/684-5709   FAX 775/684-5718
1-800/450-8594 (Toll Free)

Scott W. Anderson, Chief Deputy Secretary of State
E-Mail: scotta@sos.nv.gov
775/684-5711 FAX 775/684-5718

Wayne Thorley, Deputy Secretary of State for Elections
E-Mail: nvelect@sos.nv.gov
775/684-5705   FAX 775/684-5718

Justus Wendland, HAVA Coordinator
E-Mail: jwendland@sos.nv.gov
775/684-5705   FAX 775/684-5718

Jeff Landerfelt, Deputy Secretary of State for Commercial
      Recordings
E-Mail: jlanderfelt@sos.nv.gov
775/684-5714   FAX 775/684-5725

-Candidates on Ballot
-Election Results
-Federal Campaign Finance Reports
      (Online via FEC.gov)
-Federal Personal Financial Reports
-State Campaign Finance Reports (Online)
-PAC Registration and Finance Reports (Online)
-Ballot Advocacy Group Finance Reports (Online)
-State Personal Financial Reports of Elected
      Officials and Candidates (Online)
-Election Complaints
-Voting Accessibility

-Statewide Voter Registration System
-HAVA and the Administration of Elections

-Corporate Registration

COMMISSION ON ETHICS

Yvonne M. Nevarez-Goodson, Esq., Executive Director
Nevada Commission on Ethics
704 West Nye Lane, Suite 204
Carson City, Nevada 89703
URL http://ethics.nv.gov
E-Mail: ynevarez@ethics.nv.gov
775/687-5469   FAX 775/687-1279

      Tracy L. Chase, Esq., Commission Counsel
      E-Mail: tchase@ethics.nv.gov

-Ethics Complaints
-Advisory Opinions
-Acknowledgments
-Representation Disclosures

LEGISLATIVE REFERENCE

Richard S. Combs, Director
Legislative Counsel Bureau
401 South Carson Street
Carson City, Nevada 89701-4747
URL http://www.leg.state.nv.us/
E-Mail: admin@lcb.state.nv.us
775/684-6800   FAX 775/684-6600

-State Lobby Reports

ATTORNEY GENERAL

Adam Paul Laxalt (Elected, R)
Attorney General of Nevada
100 North Carson Street
Carson City, Nevada 89701-4717
URL http://ag.nv.gov
775/684-1100   FAX 775/684-1108

     Lawrence VanDyke, Solicitor General
     775/684-1227   FAX 775/684-1108

*
*   -Other Court Actions
*
*
*
*
*
*
*
*

NEW HAMPSHIRE

SECRETARY OF STATE

William M. Gardner (Elected by Legislature, D) Secretary of State State House, Room 204 107 North Main Street Concord, New Hampshire 03301 *URL http://sos.nh.gov* 603/271-3242 FAX 603/271-6316	-Candidates on Ballot -Election Results -Federal Personal Financial Reports -State Campaign Finance Reports -State Lobby Reports -Voting Accessibility

      Robert P. Ambrose, Senior Deputy Secretary of State
      David M. Scanlan, Deputy Secretary of State
      Karen H. Ladd, Assistant Secretary of State

Division of Archives and Records Management 71 South Fruit Street Concord, New Hampshire 03301 *URL http://sos.nh.gov/Arch_Rec_Mgmt.aspx* 603/271-2236 FAX 603/271-2272	-Federal Campaign Finance Reports (Online via FEC.gov)
Corporation Division 107 North Main Street Concord, New Hampshire 03301 *URL http://sos.nh.gov/Corp_Div.aspx* 603/271-3244 603/271-3246 (Name Availability)	-Corporate Registration

LEGISLATIVE REFERENCE

Reference and Information Services
New Hampshire State Library
20 Park Street
Concord, New Hampshire 03301
URL http://www.nh.gov/nhsl/
603/271-2144 FAX 603/271-2205

Myla Padden, Director of Research
Office of Legislative Services
State House, Room 109
107 North Main Street
Concord, New Hampshire 03301
URL http://gencourt.state.nh.us/ols
E-Mail: Myla.Padden@leg.state.nh.us
603/271-3326 FAX603/271-6607

ATTORNEY GENERAL

Joseph A. Foster (Appointed, D) Attorney General of New Hampshire 33 Capitol Street Concord, New Hampshire 03301-6397 *URL http://doj.nh.gov* 603/271-3658 FAX 603/271-2110	-Other Court Actions

      Anne M. Edwards, Associate Attorney General

DEPARTMENT OF STATE

Kim Guadagno (Elected, R)   * -Chief Election Officer
Lieutenant Governor   *
State House   *
125 West State Street, P.O. Box 300   *
Trenton, New Jersey 08625-0300   *
URL http://www.state.nj.us/state/   *
609/777-2581   FAX 609/777-1764   *
                                                             *
Robert F. Giles, Director   * -Candidates on Ballot
Division of Elections   * -Election Results
225 West State Street, 5th Floor   * -Federal Campaign Finance Reports
P.O. Box 304   *   (Online via FEC.gov)
Trenton, New Jersey 08625-0304   * -Federal Personal Financial Reports
URL http://www.Elections.NJ.gov   * -Help America Vote Act Implementation
E-Mail: njelections@sos.state.nj.us   * -National Voter Registration Act Implementation
609/292-3760 FAX 609/777-1280   * -Voting Accessibility
TTY 1-877/658-6837   *

ELECTION LAW ENFORCEMENT COMMISSION

                                                             *
Jeffrey M. Brindle, Executive Director   * -State and Local Campaign Finance Reports
New Jersey Election Law Enforcement Commission   * -State Personal Financial Reports
28 West State Street, P.O. Box 185   *   (Gubernatorial and Legislative Candidates)
Trenton, New Jersey 08625-0185   * -State Lobby Reports
URL http://www.elec.state.nj.us   * -State Public Financing Documentation
E-Mail: jeff.brindle@elec.nj.gov   * -Public Question and Financial Reporting
609/292-8700 FAX 609/777-1457   * -Pay-to-Play Disclosure
1/888-313-3532 (Toll Free in State)   *
                                                             *
    Joseph W. Donohue, Deputy Director   *
    Demery J. Roberts, Legal Director   *
    Stephanie Olivo, Compliance Director   *
    Anthony Giancarli, Director of Information Technology   *
    Shreve Marshall, Director of Review and Investigation   *
    Todd Wojcik, Associate Director of Compliance   *
    Christopher Mistichelli, Director of Finance and Administration *

STATE ETHICS COMMISSION

                                                             *
Susana E. Guerrero, Executive Director   * -State Personal Financial Reports
State Ethics Commission   *   (State Employees)
28 West State Street, Room 1407   *
P.O. Box 082   *
Trenton, New Jersey 08625-0082   *
URL http://www.nj.gov/ethics   *
E-Mail: ethics@ethics.state.nj.us   *
609/292-1892 FAX 609/633-9252   *
1-888-223-1355 (Toll Free)   *
                                                             *
    Mark T. Holmes, Esq., Deputy Director   *

LEGISLATIVE REFERENCE

Lori O'Mara-Van Driesen, Director
Office of Public Information
Office of Legislative Services
State House Annex, Room 50
P.O. Box 068
Trenton, New Jersey 08625-0068
URL http://www.njleg.state.nj.us
E-Mail: leginfo@njleg.org
609/847-3905   FAX 609/777-2440
1-800/792-8630 (Toll Free)
Hearing Impaired: Dial 711 For NJ Relay

* -Legislative Schedules and Public Information

DEPARTMENT OF THE TREASURY

Jignasa Desai-McCleary, Director
Division of Purchase and Property
33 West State Street
P.O. Box 039
Trenton, New Jersey 08625
URL http://www.state.nj.us/treasury/purchase/execorder134.shtml
609/292-4886

* -Political Contributions Compliance

Corporate Records Unit
Division of Revenue and Enterprise Services
33 West State Street
P.O. Box 450
Trenton, New Jersey 08646-0450
URL http //www.state.nj.us/treasury/revenue/dcr/programs/corprec.shtml
609/292-9292   FAX 609/984-6855

* -Corporate Registration

ATTORNEY GENERAL

Robert Lougy (Appointed, R)
Acting Attorney General of New Jersey
Department of Law and Public Safety
25 Market Street, P.O. Box 080
Trenton, New Jersey 08625-0080
URL http://www.njpublicsafety.com
609/292-4925   FAX 609/292-3508

    Rebecca Ricigliano, First Assistant Attorney General
    609/984-9504

* -Other Court Actions
* -Counsel To State Chief Election Official And New
    Jersey's County Boards of Elections and
    County Superintendents of Elections

SECRETARY OF STATE

Brad Winter (Elected, R)
Secretary of State
325 Don Gaspar, Suite 300
Santa Fe, New Mexico 87501
URL http://www.sos.state.nm.us
E-Mail: brad.winter@state.nm.us
505/827-3628 FAX 505/827-8081
1-800/477-3632 (Toll Free)

Mary Quintana, Deputy Secretary of State
E-Mail: mary.quintana2@state.nm.us
505/827-3636 FAX 505/827-8403

Kari Fresquez, Bureau of Elections Interim Director
E-Mail: kari.fresquez@state.nm.us
505/827-3622 FAX 505/827-8403

Ken Ortiz, Chief Administrator
Business Services Division
E-Mail: kenneth.ortiz@state.nm.us
505/827-3661 FAX 505/827-3611

```
*
*      -Candidates on Ballot
*      -Election Results
*      -Federal Campaign Finance Reports
*          (Online via FEC.gov)
*      -State Campaign Finance Reports
*          (Candidates and Political Action Committees)
*      -State Personal Financial Disclosure Reports
*      -Lobbyist Reports
*      -Voter Action Act
*      -Voting Accessibility
*
*
*
*
*
*
*
*
*
*      -Corporate Registration
*      -Partnership, UCC, Notary Filings
*      -Trademarks
*
```

LEGISLATIVE REFERENCE

Raúl E. Burciaga, Director
Legislative Council Service
411 State Capitol
Santa Fe, New Mexico 87501
URL http://www.nmlegis.gov
E-Mail: raul.burciaga@nmlegis.gov
505/986-4671 FAX 505/986-4680

Laurie Canepa, Senior Legislative Librarian
505/986-4667

```
*
*
*
*
*
*
*
*
*
*
*
*
```

ATTORNEY GENERAL

Hector Balderas (Elected, D)
Attorney General of New Mexico
408 Galisteo Street
Santa Fe, New Mexico 87501
URL http://www.nmag.gov
505/827-6000 FAX 505/827-5826
    Mailing Address:
    P.O. Drawer 1508
    Santa Fe, New Mexico 87504-1508

```
*
*      -Other Court Actions
*
*
*
*
*
*
*
```

SECRETARY OF STATE

Rossana Rosado (Appointed, D)
Secretary of State
One Commerce Plaza
99 Washington Avenue, 11th Floor
Albany, New York 12231
URL http://www.dos.ny.gov
E-Mail: info@dos.ny.gov
518/474-4752   FAX 518/474-4597

Sandra J. Tallman, Director
Corporations Division, 6th Floor
E-Mail: corporations@dos.ny.gov
518/473-2492 (Information)   FAX 518/473-1654

-Corporate Registration

STATE BOARD OF ELECTIONS

Todd D. Valentine, Co-Executive Director
Robert A. Brehm, Co-Executive Director
State Board of Elections
40 North Pearl Street, Suite 5
Albany, New York 12207-2729
URL http://www.elections.ny.gov
E-Mail: info@elections.ny.gov
518/474-8100   FAX 518/486-4068

    Kimberly Galvin, Co-Counsel, 518/474-6367
        E-Mail: kimberly.galvin@elections.ny.gov
    Brian Quail, Co-Counsel, 518/474-2063
        E-Mail: brian.quail@elections.ny.gov
    Risa Sugarman, Enforcement Counsel, 518/486-7858
        E-Mail: risa.sugarman@elections.ny.gov
    John Conklin, Director of Public Information, 518/474-1953
        E-Mail: john.conklin@elections.ny.gov
    Patti Lloyd, Associate Accountant, 518/474-8200
        E-Mail: patricia.lloyd@elections.ny.gov
    Anna E. Svizzero, Director of Election Operations, 518/473-5086
        E-Mail: anna.svizzero@elections.ny.gov

-Candidates on Ballot
-Election Results
-Federal Campaign Finance Reports
    (Online via FEC.gov)
-Federal Personal Financial Reports
-State and Local Campaign Finance Reports
-Voting Accessibility
-Electronic Filings
-Enrollment Statistics
-Election Law

NEW YORK CITY BOARD OF ELECTIONS

Michael J. Ryan, Executive Director
New York City Board of Elections
32 Broadway, 7th Floor
New York, New York 10004-1609
URL http://www.vote.nyc.ny.us
212/487-5403   FAX 212/487-5349
212/868-3692 or 1-866/868-3692 (Voter Information)
TTY 212/487-5496

    Dawn Sandow, Deputy Executive Director, 212/487-5412
        E-Mail: dsandow@boe.nyc.ny.us
    Pamela Green Perkins, Administrative Manager 212/487-5406
        E-Mail: pperkins@boe.nyc.ny.us
    Steven Richman, Legal Counsel, 212/487-5338
        E-Mail: srichman@boe.nyc.ny.us

-Candidates on Ballot
-Election Results
-City Campaign Finance Reports
-Public Access Terminals
-Voter Information and Services
-Voter Registration Statistics

(Continued on Next Page)

NEW YORK CITY BOARD OF ELECTIONS (Continued)

New York City Board of Elections
32 Broadway, 7th Floor
New York, New York 10004-1609
URL http://www.vote.nyc.ny.us
212/487-5403 FAX 212/487-5349
212/868-3692 or 1-866/868-3692 (Voter Information)
TTY 212/487-5496

    Raphael Savino, Deputy General Counsel/Campaign Finance
        Reporting Counsel, 212/487-5307
        E-Mail: rsavino@boe.nyc.ny.us
    Gerald Sullivan, Financial Officer, 212/487-5329
        E-Mail: gsullivan@boe.nyc.ny.us
    Valerie Vazquez, Director of Communications and Public
        Affairs, 212/487-5404
        E-Mail: vvazquez@boe.nyc.ny.us
    Beth Fossella, Coordinator of Voter Registration, 212/487-5320
        E-Mail: bfossella@boe.nyc.ny.us
    Troy Johnson, Coordinator of Candidate Records Unit
        212/487-5417
        E-Mail: tjohnson@boe.nyc.ny.us
    Georgea Kontzamanis, Operations Manager, 212/487-8648
        E-Mail: gkontzamanis@boe.nyc.ny.us

NEW YORK CITY CAMPAIGN FINANCE BOARD

Amy M. Loprest, Executive Director
New York City Campaign Finance Board
100 Church Street, 12th Floor
New York, New York 10007
URL http://www.nyccfb.info
E-Mail: info@nyccfb.info
212/409-1800 FAX 212/409-1705

    Sue Ellen Dodell, General Counsel, 212/306-7114
    Eric Friedman, Assistant Executive Director for Public Affairs
        212/306-7116
    Roberta Maria Baldini, Assistant Executive Director for
        Campaign Finance Administration, 212/409-1740
    Kitty Chan, Chief of Staff, 212/409-1870
    Daniel Cho, Director of Candidate Services, 212/306-7147
    Sauda Chapman, Director of Auditing and Accounting
        212/409-1818
    Onida Coward Mayers, Director of Voter Assistance
        212/306-7119
    Kenneth O'Brien, Director of Systems Administration
        212/306-7132
    Jesse Schaffer, Director of Special Compliance, 212/306-5229
    Matthew Sollars, Press Secretary, 212/306-5262
    Elizabeth A. Upp, Director of Communications, 212/306-7149
    Hillary Weisman, Director of Legal Unit, 212/306-7100
    Corey Schaffer, Director of Administrative Services and Human
        Resources, 212-409-1750

-City Campaign Finance Reports
    (For Candidates for Mayor,
      Public Advocate, Comptroller, Borough
      President and City Council)
-Public Financing (Voluntary)
-Online Searchable Database Enabling Customized
      Searches of Contributors, Intermediaries,
      Employers and Expenditures
-Internet Filings of Disclosure Statements
-Debate Program for Citywide Candidates
-Voter Guide
-Voter Assistance
-Disclosure Of Independent Expenditures

NEW YORK CITY CONFLICTS OF INTEREST BOARD

Carolyn Lisa Miller, Executive Director
New York City Conflicts of Interest Board
2 Lafayette Street, Suite 1010
New York, New York 10007
URL http://nyc.gov/ethics
E-Mail: miller@coib.nyc.gov
212/442-1400   FAX 212/442-1407

    Wayne G. Hawley, Deputy Executive Director and General
       Counsel, 212/442-1415
       E-Mail: hawley@coib.nyc.gov
    Varuni Bhagwant, Director of Administration, 212/442-1427
       E-Mail: bhagwant@coib.nyc.gov
    Michele Weinstat, Director of Enforcement, 212/442-1419
       E-Mail: mweinstat@coib.nyc.gov
    Julia Davis, Director of Financial Disclosure, 212/442-1445
       E-Mail:davis@coib.nyc.gov
    Alex Kipp, Director of Training and Education, 212/442-1421
       E-Mail: kipp@coib.nyc.gov
    Derick Yu, Director of Information Technology, 212/442-1605
       E-Mail: yu@coib.nyc.gov

* -Financial Disclosure Reports
* -Ethics Matters of City Public Servants

NEW YORK STATE JOINT COMMISSION ON PUBLIC ETHICS

Seth A. Agata, Executive Director
New York State Joint Commission on Public Ethics
540 Broadway
Albany, New York 12207
URL http://www.jcope.ny.gov
E-Mail: jcope@jcope.ny.gov
518/408-3976   FAX 518/408-3975

* -State Personal Financial Disclosure Reports
    (Executive and Legislative Branch Employees
    and Elected Officials, Candidates For Those
    Offices and State Political Party Chairs and
    Selected County Chairs)
* -Publications on Financial Disclosure, Gifts and
    Guides for State Employees
* -State Lobby Filings and Reports
* -Section 166 Record of Appearances
* -Local Government Lobby Filings and Reports
* -Procurement Lobbying Filings and Reports
* -Advisory Opinions
* -Investigations
* -Enforcement Proceedings

LEGISLATIVE ETHICS COMMISSION

Lisa P. Reid, Executive Director/Counsel
Legislative Ethics Commission
Box 75 LOB
Albany, New York 12247
URL http://www.legethics.com
E-Mail: lreid@nysenate.gov
518/432-7837   FAX 518/426-6850

* -State Personal Financial Reports
    (Legislators, Candidates, Employees of
    Legislature)
* -State Legislature Standards of Conduct
* -Advisory Opinions
* -Training

LEGISLATIVE REFERENCE

Legislative Library
State Capitol, Room 337
Albany, New York 12224
E-Mail: leglibry@nysenate.gov
518/455-4000   FAX 518/426-6901

ATTORNEY GENERAL

Eric T. Schneiderman (Elected, D)
Attorney General of New York
State Capitol
Albany, New York 12224-0341
URL http://www.ag.ny.gov
1-800/771-7755 (Toll Free)   FAX 518/473-9909

-Other Court Actions

SECRETARY OF STATE

Elaine Marshall (Elected, D) Secretary of State P.O. Box 29622 Raleigh, North Carolina 27626-0622 *URL http://www.sosnc.gov* 919/807-2005 FAX 919/807-2010	
Cheri L. Myers, Director Corporations Division P.O. Box 29622 Raleigh, North Carolina 27626-0622 *E-Mail: corpinfo@sosnc.com* 919/807-2225 FAX 919/807-2039	-Corporate Registration
Joal Broun, Director Lobbying Compliance Division P.O. Box 29622 Raleigh, North Carolina 27626-0622 *E-Mail: lobbyist@sosnc.com* 919/807-2170 FAX 919/807-2205	-State Lobby Reports -Enforcement of Lobbying Laws -Regulation of Lobbying, Registration and Reporting Activities -Directory of Registrations

STATE BOARD OF ELECTIONS

Kim Westbrook Strach, Executive Director
State Board of Elections
441 North Harrington Street
Raleigh, North Carolina 27603
URL http://www.ncsbe.gov
E-Mail: kim.strach@ncsbe.gov
E-Mail: elections.sboe@ncsbe.gov
919/733-7173 FAX 919/715-0135
866/522-4723
    Mailing Address:
    P.O. Box 27255
    Raleigh, North Carolina 27611-7255
 	
    Marc Burris, Information Systems Director
    E-Mail: marc.burris@ncsbe.gov
    Veronica Degraffenreid, Election Preparation & Support Manager
    E-Mail: Veronica.Degraffenreid@ncsbe.gov
    Jackie Hyland, Public Information Officer
    E-Mail: Jackie.Hyland@ncsbe.gov
    Josh Lawson, General Counsel
    E-Mail: joshua.lawson@ncsbe.gov
    Amy Strange, Deputy Director, Campaign Finance & Operations
    E-Mail: amy.strange@ncsbe.gov
	-Candidates on Ballot
	-Election Results
	-Voting Accessibility
	-Federal Campaign Finance Reports
	    (Online via FEC.gov)
	-Federal Personal Financial Reports
	-State Campaign Finance Reports
	-State Initiative/Referendum Spending Reports
	-Electronic Filings
	-Campaign Finance Education
	-Training for Campaign Treasurers

STATE ETHICS COMMISSION

Perry Y. Newson, Executive Director
North Carolina State Ethics Commission
1324 Mail Service Center
Raleigh, North Carolina 27699-1324
URL http://www.ethicscommission.nc.gov
E-Mail: ethics.commission@doa.nc.gov
919/814-3600 FAX 919/715-1644
	-Statements of Economic Interest
	    (All Branches of Government, State Boards,
	    Commissions, and Councils, and Exempt State
	    Employees)
	-Legislative Ethics and Financial Reports
	-Enforcement of Ethics and Lobbying Laws
	-Ethics and Lobbying Education

STATE TREASURER

Janet Cowell (Elected, D)
State Treasurer
325 North Salisbury Street, Suite 100
Raleigh, North Carolina 27603-1385
URL http://www.nctreasurer.com
919/508-5176 FAX 919/508-5167

-Management of Public Funds
-Administration of State and Public Employee
 Pension Funds
-Issuance of State and Local Government Bonds

DEPARTMENT OF REVENUE

Lyons Gray, Secretary of Revenue
Department of Revenue
501 North Wilmington Street
P.O. Box 871
Raleigh, North Carolina 27602-0871
URL http://www.dornc.com
919/814-1006 FAX 919/733-0023
1-877-252-3052

-Collection of Public Financing Funds

LEGISLATIVE REFERENCE

Cathy Martin, Librarian
Legislative Library
Legislative Office Building, Room 500
300 North Salisbury Street
Raleigh, North Carolina 27603-5925
URL http://www.ncleg.net/library
919/733-9390 FAX 919/715-5460

ATTORNEY GENERAL

Roy Cooper (Elected, D)
Attorney General of North Carolina
9001 Mail Service Center
Raleigh, North Carolina 27699-9001
URL http://www.ncdoj.gov
919/716-6400 FAX 919/716-0803

-Other Court Actions
-Advisory Letters and Opinions

      Katherine A. Murphy, Assistant Attorney General
      Special Litigation Division
      E-Mail: kmurphy@ncdoj.gov
      919/716-6900 FAX 919/716-6764

      Alec Peters, Senior Deputy Attorney General
      Elections Section
      E-Mail: apeters@ncdoj.gov
      919/716-6800 FAX 919/716-6755

SECRETARY OF STATE

Alvin A. (Al) Jaeger (Elected, R)	-Candidates on Ballot
Secretary of State	-Election Results
State Capitol	-Federal Campaign Finance Reports
600 East Boulevard Avenue, Dept. 108	(Online via FEC.gov)
Bismarck, North Dakota 58505-0500	-Federal Personal Financial Reports
URL http://www.sos.nd.gov	-State Campaign Finance Reports
E-Mail: sos@nd.gov	-State Personal Financial Reports
701/328-2900 FAX 701/328-3413	-State Lobby Reports
1-800/352-0867 (Toll Free)	-State Initiative/Referendum Spending Reports
	-Voting Accessibility

Jim Silrum, Deputy Secretary of State

John Arnold, Director of Elections
URL http://www.vote.nd.gov
E-Mail: soselect@nd.gov
701/328-4146 FAX 701/328-3413

Lee Ann Oliver, Elections Specialist

Business Information/Registration Division — -Business Registration
E-Mail: sosbir@nd.gov
701/328-4284 FAX 701/328-2992
TTY 1-800/366-6888

LEGISLATIVE REFERENCE

Jim W. Smith, Director — -State Legislative Ethics
Legislative Council
State Capitol
600 East Boulevard Avenue
Bismarck, North Dakota 58505-0360
URL http://www.legis.nd.gov
E-Mail: lcouncil@nd.gov
701/328-2916 FAX 701/328-3615

ATTORNEY GENERAL

Wayne Stenehjem (Elected, R) — -Other Court Actions
Attorney General of North Dakota — -State's Chief Legal Counsel
State Capitol
600 East Boulevard Avenue, Dept. 125
Bismarck, North Dakota 58505-0040
URL http://www.ag.nd.gov
E-Mail: ndag@nd.gov
701/328-2210 FAX 701/328-2226
TTY 1-800/366-6888

LIEUTENANT GOVERNOR

Victor Borja Hocog (R)
Lieutenant Governor
Office of the Governor
Commonwealth of the Northern Mariana Islands
Caller Box 10007, Capitol Hill
Saipan, MP 96950
URL http://gov.mp
670/664-2301 FAX 670/664-2311

COMMONWEALTH ELECTION COMMISSION

Julita A. Villagomez, Acting Executive Director
Commonwealth Election Commission
Commonwealth of the Northern Mariana Islands
P.O. Box 500470
Saipan, MP 96950-0470
URL http://www.votecnmi.gov.mp
E-Mail: executivedirector@votecnmi.gov.mp
670/235-8680, 670/235-8680, 670/664-8682   FAX 670/664-8689

-Candidates on Ballot
-Election Results
-Federal Campaign Finance Reports
-Federal Personal Financial Reports
-Territorial Campaign Finance Reports

OFFICE OF THE PUBLIC AUDITOR

Michael Pai, Public Auditor
CNMI Office of the Public Auditor
1236 Yap Drive, Capitol Hill
P.O. Box 501399
Saipan, MP 96950
URL http://www.opacnmi.com/sec.asp?secID=1
670/322-6481 FAX 670/322-7812

-Enforcement of the Government Ethics Code
    Act of 1992
-Oversees the Submissions of the Statements of
    Financial Interests by Reporting Individuals
-Initiates, Receives, Investigates and Issues
    Opinions on Complaints of Violations
    of the Ethics Code

DEPARTMENT OF COMMERCE

Mark O. Rabauliman, Secretary of Commerce
Office of the Registrar of Corporations
CNMI Department of Commerce
Caller Box 10007
Saipan, MP 96950
URL http://commerce.gov.mp/divisions/registrar
E-Mail: registrar.corp@commerce.gov.mp
670/664-3000 FAX 670/664-3067

-Corporate Registration

LEGISLATIVE REFERENCE

Michael A. Stanker, Executive Director
Commonwealth Law Revision Commission
Commonwealth of the Northern Mariana Islands
P.O. Box 502179
Saipan, MP 96950-2179
URL http://www.cnmilaw.org
670/236-9820 FAX 670/236-9897

-Codifies All Permanent CNMI Laws
-Publishes Decisions of the CNMI courts
-Codifies All Government Agency Regulations

ATTORNEY GENERAL

Edward Manibusan (Elected)
Attorney General
Commonwealth of the Northern Mariana Islands
Office of the Attorney General
P.O. Box 10007, Capitol Hill
Saipan, MP 96950-8907
URL http://oagcnmi.net/sec.asp?secID=1
670/664-2341   FAX 670/664-2349

*
*   -Other Court Actions
*
*
*
*
*
*

SECRETARY OF STATE

Jon Husted (Elected, R)
Secretary of State
180 East Broad Street, 16th Floor
Columbus, Ohio 43215
URL http://www.ohiosecretaryofstate.gov
E-Mail: jhusted@ohiosecretaryofstate.gov
877/767-6446   FAX 614/644-0649

> Matt Damschroder, Assistant Secretary of State and Chief of Staff
> *E-Mail: mdamschroder@ohiosecretaryofstate.gov*
> 614/728-9132   FAX 614/485-7526
> Jack Christopher, Deputy Assistant Secretary of State and Chief
>   Legal Counsel
> *E-Mail: jchristopher@ohiosecretaryofstate.gov*
> 614/466-9510   FAX 614/485-7699
> Craig Forbes, Deputy Chief of Staff
> *E-Mail: cforbes@ohiosecretaryofstate.gov*
> 614/644-1373   FAX 614/485-7591

Elections Division
180 East Broad Street, 15th Floor
Columbus, Ohio 43215
E-Mail: election@ohiosecretaryofstate.gov
614/466-2585   FAX 614/752-4360

-Candidates on Ballot
-Election Results
-Federal Campaign Finance Reports
      (Online via FEC.gov)
-Federal Personal Financial Reports
-State Campaign Finance Reports
      (Statewide Candidates, PACs and Party
      Committees)
-State Initiative/Referendum Spending Reports
-Voting Accessibility
-Electronic Filings

> Patricia Wolfe, Elections Administrator
> Laura Pietenpol, Deputy Elections Administrator
> Matthew Tlachac, Deputy Elections Administrator
> Brandi Seskes, Deputy Elections Administrator and Elections
>   Counsel
> Carolyn Kuruc, Senior Elections Counsel

Campaign Finance Division
180 East Broad Street, 16th Floor
Columbus, Ohio 43215
E-Mail: cfinance@ohiosecretaryofstate.gov
614/466-3111   FAX 614/752-4360

> Katie Zvolanek, Director of Campaign Finance and
>   Administrative Counsel
> *E-Mail: kzvolanek@ohiosecretaryofstate.gov*
> 614/728-6855   FAX 614/485-7610

Business Services Division
180 East Broad Street, 1st Floor
Columbus, Ohio 43215
E-Mail: busserv@ohiosecretaryofstate.gov
877/767-3453 (Toll Free)   FAX 614/485-7681

-Corporate Registration

> Allison DeSantis, Director of Business Services
> *E-Mail: adesantis@ohiosecretaryofstate.gov*
> 614/466-0952   FAX 614/485-7609

OHIO ELECTIONS COMMISSION

Philip Richter, Executive Director/Staff Attorney
Ohio Elections Commission
77 South High Street, Suite 1850
Columbus, Ohio 43215
URL http://elc.ohio.gov
614/466-3205   FAX 614/728-9408

-State Campaign Finance and Campaign Practices
    Enforcement

LEGISLATIVE SERVICE COMMISSION

Mark Flanders, Director
Legislative Service Commission
77 South High Street, 9th Floor
Columbus, Ohio 43215-6136
URL http://www.lsc.ohio.gov/
614/466-3615   FAX 614/644-1721

    Andrea Holmes, Division Chief, Judiciary, Criminal and Civil
       Law, and Elections
    Emily Wendel, Staff Attorney, Elections

-Legislation
-Bill Analyses
-Fiscal Analyses
-Research

JOINT LEGISLATIVE ETHICS COMMITTEE

Tony W. Bledsoe, Executive Director
Office of the Legislative Inspector General
50 West Broad Street, Suite 1308
Columbus, Ohio 43215-5908
URL http://www.jlec-olig.state.oh.us
614/728-5100

    Jennifer Lockwood, General Counsel
    E-Mail: jennifer.lockwood@jlec.state.oh.us

-State Lobby Reports
-Lobbying Reports for Legislative Agents and
    Executive Agency Lobbyists, and Retirement
    System Lobbyists
    (Including Initials and Updates)
-Lobbyist Lists (Executive, Legislative and
    Retirement) by Agent and Employer
-State Personal Financial Disclosure Reports for
    State Senators, Representatives and
    Candidates to the General Assembly
-Post-Employment Disclosure

OHIO ETHICS COMMISSION

Paul M. Nick, Executive Director
Ohio Ethics Commission
William Green Building
30 West Spring Street, L3
Columbus, Ohio 43215-2256
URL http://www.ethics.ohio.gov
E-Mail: paul.nick@ethics.ohio.gov
614/466-7090   FAX 614/466-8368

    Susan Willeke, Education and Communications Administrator
    E-Mail: susan.willeke@ethics.ohio.gov
    Julie M. Korte, Chief Investigative Attorney
    E-Mail: julie.korte@ethics.ohio.gov
    Brian Ring, IT Administrator
    E-Mail: brian.ring@ethics.ohio.gov
    Sarah Creedon, General Counsel
    E-Mail: Sarah. Creedon@ethics.ohio.gov

-State Personal Financial Disclosure Reports
    (Elected City, County and State Officials,
    Board and Commission CEO's and Members,
    Senior-Level State Employees and Officials,
    School District Board Members for
    Larger School Districts, and Superintendents,
    Treasurers and Business Managers)

BOARD OF PROFESSIONAL CONDUCT OF THE SUPREME COURT

Richard A. Dove, Director
Board of Professional Conduct of the Supreme Court
65 South Front Street, 5th Floor
Columbus, Ohio 43215-3431
URL http://www.supremecourt.ohio.gov/Boards/BOC/default.asp
614/387-9370 FAX 614/387-9379

    D. Allen Asbury, Senior Counsel

-State Personal Financial Disclosure Reports for
   Judges, Magistrates and Judicial Candidates

ATTORNEY GENERAL

Mike DeWine (Elected, R)
Attorney General of Ohio
30 East Broad Street, 17th Floor
Columbus, Ohio 43215-3428
URL http://www.ohioattorneygeneral.gov
614/466-4320 FAX 614/466-5087

    Amy Sexton, Scheduler
    614/728-4948

    Jacque King, Executive Assistant
    614/728-5458

-Other Court Actions

OKLAHOMA

SECRETARY OF STATE

Chris Benge (Appointed, R)
Secretary of State
2300 North Lincoln Boulevard, Suite 101
Oklahoma City, Oklahoma 73105-4897
URL http://www.sos.ok.gov
E-Mail: chris.benge@sos.ok.gov
405/521-6434 FAX 405/521-2031

    Chris Morriss, Assistant Secretary
    E-Mail: chris.morriss@sos.ok.gov

Business Division
405/521-6434 FAX 405/521-2031

-State Initiatives and Referendums

-Business Registrations

STATE ELECTION BOARD

Paul Ziriax, Secretary
State Election Board
2300 North Lincoln Boulevard, Room B-6
Oklahoma City, Oklahoma 73105
URL http://www.elections.ok.gov
E-Mail: info@elections.ok.gov
405/521-2391 FAX 405/521-6457
    Mailing Address:
    P.O. Box 53156
    Oklahoma City, Oklahoma 73152

    Pamela Slater, Assistant Secretary
    Bryan Dean, Public Information Officer
    E-Mail: bdean@elections.ok.gov

-Candidates on Ballot
-Election Results
-Voting Accessibility

ETHICS COMMISSION

Lee Slater, Executive Director
Ethics Commission
2300 North Lincoln Boulevard, Room B-5
Oklahoma City, Oklahoma 73105-4812
URL https://www.ok.gov/ethics
E-Mail: lee.slater@ethics.ok.gov
405/521-3451 FAX 405/521-4905

    Ashley Kemp, Deputy Director
    E-Mail: ashley.kemp@ethics.ok.gov
    Geoffrey Long, General Counsel
    E-Mail: geoffrey.long@ethics.ok.gov

-Federal Campaign Finance Reports
    (Online via FEC.gov)
-Federal Personal Financial Reports
-State Campaign Finance Reports
-State Personal Financial Reports
-State Lobby Reports
-Spending on State Initiatives and Referenda
-Electronic Filings

LEGISLATIVE REFERENCE

Jan Harrison, Chief Clerk
Oklahoma House of Representatives
2300 North Lincoln Boulevard, Suite 109
Oklahoma City, Oklahoma 73105
URL http://www.okhouse.gov
E-Mail: harrisonja@okhouse.gov
405/521-2711

ATTORNEY GENERAL

E. Scott Pruitt (Elected, R)
Attorney General of Oklahoma
313 Northeast 21st Street
Oklahoma City, Oklahoma 73105-4894
URL http://www.ok.gov/oag
405/521-3921 FAX 405/521-6246

*
* -Other Court Actions
*
*
*
*
*

OREGON

SECRETARY OF STATE

Jeanne P. Atkins (Appointed, D)
Secretary of State
136 State Capitol
Salem, Oregon 97310
URL http://sos.oregon.gov
E-Mail: oregon.sos@state.or.us
503/986-1523 FAX 503/986-1616

      Robert Taylor, Deputy Secretary of State
      503/986-1523 FAX 503/986-1616

Jim Williams, Director of Elections
255 Capitol Street, NE, Suite 501
Salem, Oregon 97310
E-Mail: elections.sos@state.or.us
503/986-1518 FAX 503/373-7414
TTY 1-800/735-2900

Peter Threlkel, Director
Corporation Division
255 Capitol Street, NE, Suite 151
Salem, Oregon 97310-1327
URL http://www.filinginoregon.com
503/986-2200

-Candidates on Ballot
-Election Results
-Federal Campaign Finance Reports
    (Online via FEC.gov)
-State Campaign Finance Reports
-State Initiative/Referendum Spending Reports
-Election Law Complaint Case Files
-Voting Accessibility
-Oregon Centralized Voter Registration (OCVR)
-Electronic Filings
-Corporate Registration

OREGON GOVERNMENT ETHICS COMMISSION

Ronald A. Bersin, Executive Director
Oregon Government Ethics Commission
3218 Pringle Road, SE, Suite 220
Salem, Oregon 97302-1544
URL http://www.oregon.gov/ogec
E-Mail: ogec.mail@state.or.us
503/378-5105 FAX 503/373-1456

-State Personal Financial Reports
-State Lobby Reports

LEGISLATIVE REFERENCE

Legislative Library and Public Access Room
900 Court Street, NE, Room 446
Salem, Oregon 97301
URL http://www.oregonlegislature.gov
E-Mail: help.leg@state.or.us
503/986-1668 FAX 503/986-1005
1-800/332-2313

ATTORNEY GENERAL

Ellen F. Rosenblum (Elected, D)
Attorney General of Oregon
1162 Court Street, NE
Salem, Oregon 97301
URL http://www.doj.state.or.us
E-Mail: attorneygeneral@doj.state.or.us
503/378-4400 FAX 503/378-4017

-Other Court Actions

PENNSYLVANIA

SECRETARY OF THE COMMONWEALTH

Pedro A. Cortés (Appointed, D)
Secretary of the Commonwealth
302 North Office Building
Harrisburg, Pennsylvania 17120-0029
URL http://www.dos.pa.gov
717/787-6458   FAX 717/787-1734

Jonathan M. Marks, Commissioner
Bureau of Commissions, Elections & Legislation
210 North Office Building
Harrisburg, Pennsylvania 17120-0029
E-Mail: RA-BCEL@pa.gov
717/787-5280   FAX 717/705-0721

    Trisha Malehorn, Manager, Campaign Finance and Lobbying
       Disclosure Division
    Jessica Mathis, Manager, Election Services Division
    Julio Peña, Manager, Notary Division

Bureau of Corporations and Charitable Organizations
206 North Office Building
Harrisburg, Pennsylvania 17120
E-Mail: RA-CORPS@pa.gov, RA-CHARITY@pa.gov
717/787-1057   FAX 717/783-2244

-Candidates on Ballot
-Election Results
-Federal Campaign Finance Reports
    (Online via FEC.gov)
-Federal Personal Financial Reports
-State Campaign Finance Reports
-State Lobbying Disclosure Reports
-State Initiative/Referendum Spending
-Electronic Filings
-Voter Registration
-Notary Appointments
-Polling Place Accessibility

-Corporate Registration

STATE ETHICS COMMISSION

Robert P. Caruso
Executive Director
State Ethics Commission
Finance Building, Room 309
Harrisburg, Pennsylvania 17120
URL http://www.ethics.pa.gov
E-Mail: ra-ethicswebmaster@pa.gov
717/783-1610   FAX 717/787-0806
1-800/932-0936 (Toll Free)
    Mailing Address:
    P.O. Box 11470
    Harrisburg, Pennsylvania 17108-1470

-Statements of Financial Interests
-Public Orders, Opinions, Advice and Rulings
- Conflicts of Interest Investigations

LEGISLATIVE REFERENCE BUREAU

Legislative Reference Bureau
641 Main Capitol Building
Harrisburg, Pennsylvania 17120-0033
717/787-4223   FAX 717/783-2396

-Bill Status

STATE LEGISLATURE

Megan Martin, Secretary of the Senate
462 Main Capitol Building
Harrisburg, Pennsylvania 17120
URL http://www.pasen.gov
717/787-5920 FAX 717/772-2344

-Legislative Schedules and Procedures

Anthony Frank Barbush, Chief Clerk of the House
129 Main Capitol Building
P.O. Box 202220
Harrisburg, Pennsylvania 17120-2220
URL http://www.legis.state.pa.us
717/787-2372 FAX 717/787-4990

-Legislative Schedules and Procedures

PHILADELPHIA BOARD OF ETHICS

J. Shane Creamer, Jr., Esq.
Executive Director
Philadelphia Board of Ethics
One Parkway Building
1515 Arch Street, 18th Floor
Philadelphia, Pennsylvania 19102
URL: http://www.phila.gov/ethicsboard
E-Mail: shane.creamer@phila.gov
215/686-9450 FAX 215/686-9453

Nedda Massar, Deputy Executive Director
E-Mail: nedda.massar@phila.gov
Michael Cooke, Esq., Director of Enforcement
E-Mail: michael.cooke@phila.gov
Maya Nayak, Esq., General Counsel
E-mail: maya.nayak@phila.gov

-City Campaign Finance Guide
- City Campaign Finance Reports
- City Lobbying Disclosure FAQs
- City Lobbying Disclosure Reports
- City Personal Financial Disclosure FAQs
- City Public Integrity Laws and Board of Ethics
  Regulations
- Advisory Opinions
-Settlement Agreements

PHILADELPHIA CITY DEPARTMENT OF RECORDS

James Leonard, Esq.
Records Commissioner
City Hall, Room 156
Philadelphia, Pennsylvania 19107
URL http://www.phila.gov/records
E-Mail: records.info@phila.gov
215/686-2261 FAX 215/686-2273

-City Personal Financial Disclosure Reports
- Campaign Finance Reports

ATTORNEY GENERAL

Kathleen G. Kane (Elected, D)
Attorney General of Pennsylvania
Strawberry Square, 16th Floor
Harrisburg, Pennsylvania 17120
URL http://www.attorneygeneral.gov
717/787-3391 FAX 717/787-8242

-Other Court Actions

SECRETARY OF STATE

	*
Victor Suárez Meléndez (Appointed, PDP)	* -Lobbyist Registration
Secretary of State	* -Lobby Reports
P.O. Box 9023271	* -Corporate Registration
San Juan, Puerto Rico 00902-3271	*
URL http://www.estado.gobierno.pr	*
E-Mail: secretario@estado.pr.gov	*
787/722-2121 FAX 787/725-2684	*

STATE ELECTIONS COMMISSION

	*
Liza M. García Vélez	* -Candidates on Ballot
President	* -Election Results
State Elections Commission	* -Voting Accessibility
P.O. Box 195552	* -Election Administration
San Juan, Puerto Rico 00919-5552	* -State Personal Financial Reports
URL http://www.ceepur.org	*
787/777-8682 FAX 787/296-0173	*
	*
Guillermo San Antonio Acha, Commissioner (PDP)	*
Jorge L. Dávila Torres, Commissioner (NPP)	*
Roberto I. Aponte Berrios, Commissioner (PIP)	*
José F. Córdova Iturregui, Commissioner (PPT)	*
	*
Walter Vélez Martínez, Secretary	*
787/294-1190 FAX 787/294-1191 or 787/294-1183	*
	*
Press Office	*
787/296-0524, 787/221-4972 FAX 787/296-0419	*

OFFICE OF THE ELECTORAL COMPTROLLER

	*
Manuel A. Torres Nieves	* -Federal Campaign Finance Reports
Electoral Comptroller	* -Federal Personal Financial Reports
Office of the Electoral Comptroller	* -State Campaign Finance Reports
235 Arterial Hostos Avenue	* -State Public Financing Documentation
Capital Center Building	*
North Tower, Box 1401	*
San Juan, Puerto Rico 00918-1879	*
URL http://contralorelectoral.gov.pr	*
E-Mail: mtorres@contralorelectoral.gov.pr	*
787/332-2050, ext. 2553 FAX 787/332-2063	*

DEPARTMENT OF THE TREASURY

	*
Juan Zaragoza Gómez, Secretary	*
Department of the Treasury	* -State Public Financing Documentation
P.O. Box 9024140	*
San Juan, Puerto Rico 00902-4140	*
URL http://www.hacienda.pr.gov	*
E-Mail: info@hacienda.pr.gov	*
787/721-2020 FAX 787/721-2111	*
Taxpayer Services: 787/722-0216	*

OFFICE OF GOVERNMENT ETHICS

Zulma R. Rosario Vega, Esq., Executive Director
Office of Government Ethics of Puerto Rico
108 Ganges Street
San Juan, Puerto Rico 00926-2906
URL http://tmp.oegpr.net
E-Mail: etica@oeg.gobierno.pr
787/999-0246   FAX 787/999-0270

-State Personal Financial Reports
    (Public Officials, State Employees)
-Complaints Investigations
-Advisory Opinions

LEGISLATIVE REFERENCE

Tania Barbarossa, Secretary of the Senate
Puerto Rico Senate
The Capitol
P.O. Box 9023431
San Juan, Puerto Rico 00902-3431
URL http://www.senadopr.us
E-Mail: Webmaster@senado.pr.gov
787/724-2030, ext. 2266/2267   FAX 787/723-5413
1-800/981-2036

-Legislative Ethics and Financial Reports

Ayleen Figueroa Vázquez, Esq., Secretary of the House
Puerto Rico House of Representatives
The Capitol
P.O. Box 9022228
San Juan, Puerto Rico 00902-2228
URL http://www.tucamarapr.org/dnncamara
E-Mail: info@camaraderepresentantes.org
787/721-6040   FAX 787/723-2717

ATTORNEY GENERAL

César R. Miranda Rodríguez (Appointed, PDP)
Attorney General of Puerto Rico
Puerto Rico Department of Justice
P.O. Box 9020192
San Juan, Puerto Rico 00902-0082
URL http://www.justicia.gobierno.pr
787/721-2900   FAX 787/724-4770

-Other Court Actions

DEPARTMENT OF STATE

Nellie M. Gorbea (Elected, D)
Secretary of State
217 State House
82 Smith Street
Providence, Rhode Island 02903
URL http://www.sos.ri.gov
E-Mail: secretarygorbea@sos.ri.gov
401/222-2357 FAX 401/222-1356

Rob Rock, Director   -Candidates on Ballot
Elections Division   -Federal Campaign Finance Reports
148 West River Street   (Online via FEC.gov)
Providence, Rhode Island 02904-2615   -Voter Education and Outreach
E-Mail: rrock@sos.ri.gov
401/222-2340 FAX 401/222-1444

Stacy DiCola, Director   -State Lobby Reports
Public Information Division
Room 38, State House
82 Smith Street
Providence, Rhode Island 02903
E-Mail: sdicola@sos.ri.gov
410/222-3983 FAX 401/222-1404

Maureen Ewing, Director   -Corporate Registration
Business Services Division
148 West River Street
Providence, Rhode Island 02904
E-Mail: mewing@sos.ri.gov
401/222-3040 FAX 401/222-1309

STATE BOARD OF ELECTIONS

William E. West, Acting Chairman
Rhode Island Board of Elections
50 Branch Avenue
Providence, Rhode Island 02904
URL http://www.elections.ri.gov
E-Mail: boe.elections@elections.ri.gov
401/222-2345 FAX 401/222-3135
TDD 401/222-2239

Robert Kando, Executive Director
E-Mail: robert.kando@elections.ri.gov
401/222-2345 FAX 401/222-3135

Robert B. Rapoza, Director of Elections   -Election Results
E-Mail: robert.rapoza@elections.ri.gov   -Voting Accessibility
401/222-2345 FAX 401/222-3135   -Conduct of Elections and Voter Registration

Richard E. Thornton, Director of Campaign Finance   -State Campaign Finance Reports
E-Mail: richard.thornton@elections.ri.gov
401/222-2345 FAX 401/222-3135

RHODE ISLAND ETHICS COMMISSION

Kent A. Willever, Executive Director
Rhode Island Ethics Commission
40 Fountain Street
Providence, Rhode Island 02903
URL http://www.ethics.ri.gov
E-Mail: ethics.email@ethics.ri.gov
401/222-3790 FAX 401/222-3382

-State Personal Financial Reports

LEGISLATIVE REFERENCE

Thomas Evans, State Librarian
State Library
208 State House
82 Smith Street
Providence, Rhode Island 02903
URL http://www.sos.ri.gov/library
E-Mail: tevans@sos.ri.gov
401/222-2473 FAX 401/222-3034

-Election/Campaign Finance Laws

GENERAL TREASURER

Seth Magaziner (Elected, D)
General Treasurer
102 State House
82 Smith Street
Providence, Rhode Island 02903
URL http://www.treasury.ri.gov
E-Mail: generaltreasurer@treasury.ri.gov
401/222-2397 FAX 401/222-6140

-Maintenance and Distribution of Public Financing
 Funds

TAX ADMINISTRATOR

Marilyn Shannon McConaghy, Acting Director
Division of Taxation
Department of Revenue
One Capitol Hill
Providence, Rhode Island 02908-5800
URL http://www.tax.ri.gov
401/574-8922 FAX 401/574-8917

-Collection of Tax Check-off Funds for Public
 Financing System

ATTORNEY GENERAL

Peter F. Kilmartin (Elected, D)
Attorney General of Rhode Island
150 South Main Street
Providence, Rhode Island 02903
URL http://www.riag.ri.gov
401/274-4400, ext. 2339 FAX 401/222-1302

-Other Court Actions

SOUTH CAROLINA

SECRETARY OF STATE

Mark Hammond (Elected, R)
Secretary of State
Edgar Brown Building, Suite 525
1205 Pendleton Street
Columbia, South Carolina 29201
URL http://www.scsos.com
803/734-2170 FAX 803/734-1661
    Mailing Address:
      1205 Pendleton Street, Suite 525
      Columbia, South Carolina 29201

Division of Business Filings
803/734-2158 FAX 803/734-1614

-Administrator and Regulator of Charities Under
    the Solicitation of Charitable Funds Act
-Custodian of Acts Ratified Each Year by the
    General Assembly
-Handles the Publication of Positions within
    Certain Statewide Boards and Commissions

-Corporate Registration

STATE ELECTION COMMISSION

Marci B. Andino, Executive Director
State Election Commission
1122 Lady Street, Suite 500
Columbia, South Carolina 29201
URL http://www.scvotes.org
E-Mail: elections@elections.sc.gov
803/734-9060 FAX 803/734-9366
    Mailing Address:
    P.O. Box 5987
    Columbia, South Carolina 29250-5987

    Howard Snider, Director of Voter Services
    Janet Reynolds, Director of Administration and Finance
    Chris Whitmire, Director of Public Information and Training

-Candidates on Ballot
-Election Results
-Federal Campaign Finance Reports
    (Online via FEC.gov)
-Federal Personal Financial Reports
-Statewide Voter Registration Database
-Voting Accessibility

STATE ETHICS COMMISSION

Herbert R. Hayden, Jr., Executive Director
State Ethics Commission
5000 Thurmond Mall, Suite 250
Columbia, South Carolina 29201
URL http://ethics.sc.gov
803/253-4192 FAX 803/253-7539

    Ami R. Franklin, Assistant Director, Administration

-State Campaign Disclosure Reports (Online)
-State Personal Financial Reports (Online)
-State Lobby Reports (Online)
-Enforcement of Ethics, Campaign Finance and
    Lobbying Laws

LEGISLATIVE REFERENCE

James H. Harrison, Commissioner and Director
Legislative Council
State House
P.O. Box 11489
Columbia, South Carolina 29211
URL http://www.scstatehouse.gov
E-Mail: LegisCouncil@SCStatehouse.gov
803/212-4500 FAX 803/212-4501 (Dennis Building)

    Lena Lee, Research Librarian and Human Resources

STATE LEGISLATURE

Senator Luke A. Rankin, Chairman   -State Campaign Finance and Limited Personal
Senate Ethics Committee   Financial Reports of Senate Members and
205 Gressette Building   Candidates
Columbia, South Carolina 29201
URL http://www.scstatehouse.gov/senate.php
E-Mail: sethicscomm@scsenate.gov
803/212-6410   FAX 803/212-6499
     Mailing Address:
     P.O. Box 142
     Columbia, South Carolina 29202

Representative Kenneth A. "Kenny" Bingham, Chairman   -State Campaign Finance and Personal Financial
House Ethics Committee   Reports of House Members and Candidates
519 Blatt Building
Columbia, South Carolina 29201
URL http://www.scstatehouse.gov/house.php
E-Mail: hethicscomm@schouse.gov
803/734-3114   FAX 803/734-8795
     Mailing Address:
     P.O. Box 11867
     Columbia, SC 29211

ATTORNEY GENERAL

Alan Wilson (Elected, R)   -Other Court Actions
Attorney General of South Carolina
Rembert C. Dennis Building
1000 Assembly Street, Suite 519
Columbia, South Carolina 29201
URL http://www.scag.gov
E-Mail: infor@scattorneygeneral.com
803/734-3970   FAX 803/734-3646
     Mailing Address:
     P.O. Box 11549
     Columbia, South Carolina 29211-1549

SOUTH DAKOTA

SECRETARY OF STATE

Shantel Krebs (Elected, R)
Secretary of State
State Capitol Building, Suite 204
500 East Capitol Avenue
Pierre, South Dakota 57501-5070
URL http://www.sdsos.gov
E-Mail: sdsos@state.sd.us
605/773-3537   FAX 605/773-6580

    Kea Warne, Deputy Secretary of State, Elections Services
    Christine Lehrkamp, State Election Coordinator
    E-Mail: elections@state.sd.us
    605/773-3537   FAX: 605/773-6580

Corporations Division
E-Mail: corporations@state.sd.us
605/773-4845   FAX 605/773-4550

* -Candidates on Ballot
* -Election Results
* -Federal Campaign Finance Reports
*   (Online via FEC.gov)
* -Federal Personal Financial Interest Statements
* -State Campaign Finance Reports
* -State Personal Financial Interest Statements
* -State Lobby Reports
* -State Initiative/Referendum Campaign Finance
*   Reports

-Corporate Registration

LEGISLATIVE REFERENCE

Jason Hancock, Director
Legislative Research Council
State Capitol Building, 3rd Floor
500 East Capitol Avenue
Pierre, South Dakota 57501-5070
URL http://legis.sd.gov
E-Mail: jason.hancock@state.sd.us
605/773-3251   FAX 605/773-4576

ATTORNEY GENERAL

Marty J. Jackley (Elected, R)
Attorney General of South Dakota
1302 East Highway 14, Suite 1
Pierre, South Dakota 57501-8501
URL http://atg.sd.gov
E-Mail: atghelp@state.sd.us
605/773-3215   FAX 605/773-4106

-Other Court Actions

SECRETARY OF STATE

*
Tre Hargett (Elected by Legislature, R)　*
Secretary of State　*
State Capitol, 1st Floor　*
Nashville, Tennessee 37243-1102　*
URL http://sos.tn.gov　*
615/741-2819 FAX 615/741-5962　*
*
　　Tawnie Mathieu, Executive Assistant　*
　　E-Mail: tawnie.mathieu@tn.gov　*
*
Mark Goins, Coordinator of Elections　*　　-Candidates on Ballot
Elections Division　*　　-Election Results
312 Rosa L. Parks Avenue　*　　-Voting Accessibility
7th Floor, William R. Snodgrass Tower　*　　-Cancellations of Voter Registration
Nashville, Tennessee 37243　*
URL: http://sos.tn.gov/elections　*
E-Mail: tennessee.elections@tn.gov　*
615/741-7956 FAX 615/741-1278　*
*
　　Beth Henry-Robertson, Assistant Coordinator　*
　　Kathy Summers, Elections Specialist　*
　　615/741-7956 FAX 615/741-1278　*
*
Steve Griffy, Information Systems Manager　*
615/741-7956 FAX 615/741-1278　*
*
Nathan Burton, Director　*　　-Corporate Registration
Business Services Division　*
312 Rosa L. Parks Avenue　*
6th Floor, William R. Snodgrass Tower　*
Nashville, Tennessee 37243　*
URL: http://sos.tn.gov/business-services　*
E-Mail: Business.Services@tn.gov　*
615/741-2286 FAX 615/741-7310　*

BUREAU OF ETHICS AND CAMPAIGN FINANCE

*
Drew Rawlins, Executive Director　*
Bureau of Ethics and Campaign Finance　*
404 James Robertson Parkway, Suite 104　*
Nashville, Tennessee 37243　*
E-Mail: drew.rawlins@tn.gov　*
615/741-7959 FAX 615/532-8905　*
*
　　Janet Williams, Bureau Operations Supervisor　*
　　E-Mail: janet.williams@tn.gov　*
　　John Allyn, Legal Counsel　*
　　E-Mail: john.b.allyn@tn.gov　*

(Continued on Next Page)

BUREAU OF ETHICS AND CAMPAIGN FINANCE (Continued)

Registry of Election Finance
URL http://www.tn.gov/tref
E-Mail: registry.info@tn.gov
615/741-7959   FAX 615/532-8905

Ethics Commission
URL http://www.tn.gov/tec
E-Mail: ethics.counsel@tn.gov
615/741-7959   FAX 615/532-8905

*
*
*
*
*
*
*
*
*
*

-Federal Campaign Finance Reports
   (Online via FEC.gov)
-Federal Personal Financial Reports
-State Campaign Finance Reports

-State Personal Financial Reports
-State Lobby Reports

LEGISLATIVE REFERENCE

Charles Sherrill, State Librarian and Archivist
Tennessee State Library and Archives
403 Seventh Avenue North
Nashville, Tennessee 37243-0312
URL http://sos.tn.gov/tsla
E-Mail: reference.tsla@tn.gov
615/741-2764   FAX 615/253-6471

*
*
*
*
*
*
*
*

ATTORNEY GENERAL

Herbert H. Slatery III (Appointed by Supreme Court, R)
Attorney General of Tennessee
P.O. Box 20207
Nashville, Tennessee 37202-0207
URL http://attorneygeneral.tn.gov
615/741-3491   FAX 615/741-2009

*
*
*
*
*
*
*

-Other Court Actions

SECRETARY OF STATE

Carlos H. Cascos (Appointed, R)
Secretary of State
State Capitol, Room 1E.8
Austin, Texas 78701
URL http://www.sos.state.tx.us
E-Mail: secretary@sos.texas.gov
512/463-5770   FAX 512/475-2761
    Mailing Address:
    P.O. Box 12887
    Austin, Texas 78711-2887

Coby Shorter, III, Deputy Secretary of State
E-Mail: cshorter@sos.texas.gov
512/463-5770   FAX 512/475-2761

Lindsey Wolf, General Counsel
E-Mail: generalcounsel@sos.texas.gov
512/463-5770   FAX 512/475-2761

Keith Ingram, Director of Elections   -Candidates on Ballot
Elections Division   -Election Results
Office of the Secretary of State   -Voting Accessibility
1019 Brazos Street
Austin, Texas 78701
URL http://www.sos.state.tx.us/elections/index.shtml
E-Mail: elections@sos.texas.gov
512/463-5650   FAX 512/475-2811
1-800/252-8683 (Toll Free)
TTY 7-1-1
    Mailing Address:
    P.O. Box 12060
    Austin, Texas 78711-2060

    Ashley Fischer, General Law Section
    Dan Glotzer, Election Funds Management
    Louri O'Leary, Elections Administration
    Betsy Schonhoff, Voter Registration

Corporations Section   -Corporate Registration
1019 Brazos Street
Austin, Texas 78701
URL http://www.sos.state.tx.us/corp/index.shtml
E-Mail: corphelp@sos.texas.gov
512/463-5555   FAX 512/463-5709
    Mailing Address:
    P.O. Box 13697
    Austin, Texas 78711

    Carmen Flores, Director of Business and Public Filings

TEXAS ETHICS COMMISSION

Natalia Luna Ashley, Executive Director	* -Federal Campaign Finance Reports
Texas Ethics Commission	* (Online via FEC.gov)
201 East 14th Street, 10th Floor	* -Federal Personal Financial Reports
Austin, Texas 78701	* -State Campaign Finance Reports
URL http://www.ethics.state.tx.us	* -State Personal Financial Reports
512/463-5800 FAX 512/463-5777	* -State Lobby Reports
Disclosure Filing FAX: 512/463-8808	* -Electronic Filings

Mailing Address:
P.O. Box 12070
Austin, Texas 78711-2070

LEGISLATIVE REFERENCE LIBRARY

Mary L. Camp, Director
Legislative Reference Library
1100 North Congress Avenue, Room 2N.3
P.O. Box 12488
Austin, Texas 78711-2488
URL http://www.lrl.state.tx.us
E-Mail: lrl.service@lrl.state.tx.us
512/463-1252 FAX 512/475-4626

TEXAS LEGISLATIVE COUNCIL

Legislative Redistricting Services
Research Division
Texas Legislative Council
P.O. Box 12128
Austin, Texas 78711-2128
URL http://www.tlc.state.tx.us/redist/redist.html
512/463-6622 FAX 512/936-1020

-Redistricting Support for the State Legislature

ATTORNEY GENERAL

Ken Paxton (Elected, R)
Attorney General of Texas
300 West 15th Street
Austin, Texas 78701
URL http://www.oag.state.tx.us
512/463-2191 FAX 512/475-2994
Mailing Address:
P.O. Box 12548
Austin, Texas 78711-2548

-Other Court Actions

UTAH

LIEUTENANT GOVERNOR

Spencer J. Cox (Appointed, R)
Lieutenant Governor
Office of the Lieutenant Governor
State Capitol
P.O. Box 142325
350 North State Street, Suite 220
Salt Lake City, Utah 84114-2325
URL http://www.utah.gov/ltgovernor/
801/538-1041   FAX 801/538-1133

Mark Thomas, Chief Deputy and Director of Elections
E-Mail: elections@utah.gov
801/538-1041   FAX 801/538-1133
1-800/995-8683 (Toll Free in State)

*
*   -Candidates on Ballot
*   -Election Results
*   -Federal Campaign Finance Reports
*   (Online via FEC.gov)
*   -State Campaign Finance Reports
*   -State Lobby Registration and Financial Disclosure
*   Reports
*   -State Political Party Financial Reports
*   -State Political Action and Political Issue
*   Committee Financial Reports
*   -State Corporation Financial Reports
*   -Voting Accessibility
*   -Electronic Filings
*

DEPARTMENT OF COMMERCE

Division of Corporations and Commercial Code
Department of Commerce
160 East 300 South, 2nd Floor
Salt Lake City, Utah 84111
URL http://www.corporations.utah.gov
E-Mail: corpucc@utah.gov
801/530-4849   FAX 801/530-6438
1-877/526-3994 (Toll Free in State)
    Mailing Address:
    Division of Corporations & Commercial Code
    P.O. Box 146705
    Salt Lake City, Utah 84114-6705

*
*   -Corporate and Business Registration
*   -Central Filing Office for Financing
*   Statements under the Uniform Commercial
*   Code
*
*
*
*
*
*
*
*

STATE TREASURER

David Damschen (Appointed, R)
State Treasurer
350 North State Street, Suite 180
P.O. Box 142315
Salt Lake City, Utah 84114-2315
URL http://www.treasurer.utah.gov
801/538-1042   FAX 801/538-1465

*
*   -Custody and Investment of Public Funds
*   -Member of the State Board of Canvassers
*
*
*
*
*

STATE TAX COMMISSION

John L. Valentine, Chair
Utah State Tax Commission
210 North 1950 West
Salt Lake City, Utah 84134
URL http://www.tax.utah.gov
801/297-2200   FAX 801/297-7699
1-800/662-4335 (Toll Free)

*
*   -Collection of Tax Revenue for the State
*   (and Public Financing Funds)
*
*
*
*
*

LEGISLATIVE REFERENCE

Michael Christensen, Director
Office of Legislative Research and General Counsel
West 210 House Building
State Capitol Complex
Salt Lake City, Utah 84114
URL http://le.utah.gov
801/538-1032 FAX 801/538-1712

ATTORNEY GENERAL

Sean D. Reyes (Elected, R)
Attorney General of Utah
P.O. Box 142320
Salt Lake City, Utah 84114-2320
URL http://www.attorneygeneral.utah.gov
E-Mail: uag@utah.gov
801/538-9600   FAX 801/538-1121

-Member of the State Board of Canvassers
-Legal Opinions
-Other Court Actions

VERMONT

SECRETARY OF STATE

James C. Condos (Elected, D)
Secretary of State
128 State Street
Montpelier, Vermont 05633-1101
URL http://www.sec.state.vt.us
E-Mail: secretary@sec.state.vt.us
802/828-2363   FAX 802/828-2496

    Christopher Winters, Deputy Secretary of State
       E-Mail: chris.winters@sec.state.vt.us
       802/828-2363   FAX 802/828-2496

    Will Senning, Director of Campaign Finance and Elections
       E-Mail: will.senning@sec.state.vt.us
       802/828-2363   FAX 802/828-5171

Tanya Marshall, State Archivist
1078 Route 2, Middlesex
Montpelier, VT 05633-7701
E-Mail: tanya.marshall@sec.state.vt.us
802/828-3700   FAX 802/828-3710

Marlene Betit, Director
Corporations
128 State Street
Montpelier, Vermont 05633-1101
E-Mail: corp@sec.state.vt.us
802/828-2386   FAX 802/828-2853

Colin Benjamin, Director
Office of Professional Regulation
89 Main Street, 3rd Floor
Montpelier, Vermont 05620-7701
E-Mail: colin.benjamin@sec.state.vt.us
802/828-1505   FAX 802/828-2368

- Candidates on Ballot
- Election Results
- Federal Campaign Finance Reports (Online via FEC.gov)
- Federal Personal Financial Reports
- State Campaign Finance Reports
- State Lobby Reports
- Voting Accessibility

- Archival Management
- Government Records
- Historical Research

- Corporate Registration

- Licensing

LEGISLATIVE REFERENCE

Legislative Council
115 State Street, State House
Montpelier, Vermont 05633-5301
URL http://legislature.vermont.gov (Legislature Page)
E-Mail: legcon@leg.state.vt.us
802/828-2231   FAX 802/828-2424

    Luke Martland, Director and Chief Counsel

ATTORNEY GENERAL

William H. Sorrell (Elected, D)
Attorney General of Vermont
109 State Street
Montpelier, Vermont 05609-1001
URL http://www.ago.vermont.gov
E-Mail: atginfo@atg.state.vt.us
802/828-3171   FAX 802/828-3187
TTY 802/828-3665

- Other Court Actions

VIRGINIA

SECRETARY OF THE COMMONWEALTH

Kelly Thomasson (Appointed, D)
Secretary of the Commonwealth
Patrick Henry Building
1111 East Broad Street, 4th Floor
Richmond, Virginia 23219
URL http://www.commonwealth.virginia.gov
E-Mail: socmail@governor.virginia.gov
804/786-2441 FAX 804/371-0017
    Mailing Address:
    P.O. Box 2454
    Richmond, Virginia 23218-2454

-Statements of Economic Interest
    (Statewide Office Incumbents and Candidates,
    State Employees, Board and Commission
    Members, and Judges)
-Report of the Secretary of the Commonwealth
-State Lobbyist Registration and Reports (Online)
-Gubernatorial Board and Commission
    Appointments
-Service of Process
-Authentication
-Clemency, Extraditions
-Notary

DEPARTMENT OF ELECTIONS

Edgardo Cortés, Commissioner
Virginia Department of Elections
Washington Building
1100 Bank Street, First Floor
Richmond, Virginia 23219
URL http://elections.virginia.gov
E-Mail (General Questions): info@elections.virginia.gov
E-Mail: (Campaign Finance): cfda@elections.virginia.gov
804/864-8901 FAX 804/371-0194
1-800/552-9745 (Toll Free)
TDD 804/786-0164

James B. Alcorn, Esq., Chairman, State Board of Elections
Clara Belle Wheeler, Vice Chair, State Board of Elections
Singleton B. McAllister, Esq., Secretary, State Board of Elections

-Candidates on Ballot
-Election Results
-Federal Campaign Finance Reports
    (Online via FEC.gov)
-Federal Personal Financial Reports
-State Campaign Finance Reports
-Voting Accessibility
-Electronic Filings

STATE CORPORATION COMMISSION

Joel H. Peck, Clerk of the Commission
State Corporation Commission
Tyler Building
1300 East Main Street, 1st Floor
Richmond, Virginia 23219
URL http://www.scc.virginia.gov
E-Mail: joel.peck@scc.virginia.gov
804/371-9834 FAX 804/371-9912
    Mailing Address:
    P.O. Box 1197
    Richmond, Virginia 23218-1197

-Corporate and Other Business Entity Registrations
-UCC Financing Statements

STATE LEGISLATURE

Susan Clarke Schaar
Clerk of the Senate
P.O. Box 396
Richmond, Virginia 23218
URL http://virginiageneralassembly.gov
E-Mail: sschaar@senate.virginia.gov
804/698-7400 FAX 804/698-7670

-State Personal Financial Reports of
    Senate Candidates

(Continued on Next Page)

STATE LEGISLATURE (Continued)

G. Paul Nardo Clerk of the Virginia House of Delegates P.O. Box 406 Richmond, Virginia 23218 *URL http://virginiageneralassembly.gov* *E-Mail: hics@house.virginia.gov* 804/698-1619 FAX 804/698-1800	-State Personal Financial Reports of House of Delegates Candidates

LEGISLATIVE REFERENCE

Mark J. Vucci, Acting Director Division of Legislative Services General Assembly Building 201 North Ninth Street, 2nd Floor Richmond, Virginia 23219 *URL http://dls.virginia.gov* *E-Mail: rtavenner@dls.virginia.gov* 804/786-3591, ext. 233 FAX 804/371-0169	-Drafting of Legislation and Amendments -Research and Legal Review -State Legislative District Maps, Equivalency Files and Statistics -Bill Status

      Jack Austin, Section Manager
      David Cotter, Senior Attorney
      Meg Burruss, Staff Attorney

ATTORNEY GENERAL

Mark R. Herring (Elected, D) Attorney General of Virginia Pocahontas Building 900 East Main Street Richmond, Virginia 23219 *URL http://www.ag.virginia.gov* *E-Mail: mail@oag.state.va.us* 804/786-2071 FAX 804/786-1991	-Other Court Actions

VIRGIN ISLANDS

LIEUTENANT GOVERNOR

Osbert E. Potter (Elected, I)
Lieutenant Governor
1131 King Street, Suite 101
Christiansted
St. Croix, U.S. Virgin Islands 00820
URL http://ltg.gov.vi
340/774-2991 FAX 340/774-6953
    Mailing Address:
    5049 Kongens Gade
    St. Thomas, VI 00802-6487

    Denise Johannes, Director   -Corporate Registration
    Division of Corporations and Trademarks
    E-Mail: denise.johannes@lgo-vi.gov
    340/776-8515 FAX 340/776-4612

SUPERVISOR OF ELECTIONS

Caroline F. Fawkes   -Candidates on Ballot
Supervisor of Elections   -Election Results
93A Diamond Sunny Isle Annex Unit 4   -Federal Campaign Finance Reports
Christiansted   (Online via FEC.gov)
St. Croix, U.S. Virgin Islands 00823   -Federal Personal Financial Reports
URL http://www.vivote.gov   -Local Campaign Disclosure Reporting
E-Mail: esvi.info@vi.gov   -Initiatives and Referenda
340/773-1021 FAX 340/773-4523
    Mailing Address:
    P.O. Box 1499
    Kingshill
    St. Croix, U.S. Virgin Islands 00851-1499

    Genevieve Whitaker, Deputy Supervisor of Elections, St. Croix
    340/773-1021

Kevermay Douglas, Deputy Supervisor of Elections
St. Thomas and St. John
9200 Lockhart Garden Shopping Center
P.O. Box 6038
Charlotte Amalie
St. Thomas, U.S. Virgin Islands 00804-6038
340/774-3107 FAX 340/776-2391

LEGISLATIVE REFERENCE

Colette White-Amaro, Chief Archivist
Legislature of the Virgin Islands
Capitol Building, Charlotte Amalie
St. Thomas, U.S. Virgin Islands 00804
URL http://www.legvi.org
340/774-0880 FAX 340/693-3659
    Mailing Address:
    P.O. Box 1690
    Charlotte Amalie
    St. Thomas, Virgin Islands 00804-1690

DEPARTMENT OF JUSTICE

Claude Walker, Esq. (Appointed)
Acting Attorney General of the U.S. Virgin Islands
Department of Justice
34-38 Kronprindsens Gade
GERS Complex, 2nd Floor
Charlotte Amalie
St. Thomas, U.S. Virgin Islands 00802
URL http://usvidoj.codemeta.com
340/774-5666 (ext. 107)   FAX 340/774-9710

    Pamela Tepper, Solicitor General
    Solicitor General Division
    Department of Justice
    34-38 Kronprindsens Gade
    GERS Complex, 2nd Floor
    Charlotte Amalie
    St. Thomas, U.S. Virgin Islands 00802
    340/774-5666 (ext. 118)   FAX 340/776-3494

*   -Territorial Personal Financial Reports
*   -Other Court Actions

SECRETARY OF STATE

Kim Wyman (Elected, R)
Secretary of State
Legislative Building
P.O. Box 40220
Olympia, Washington 98504-0220
URL http://www.sos.wa.gov
E-Mail: kim.wyman@sos.wa.gov
360/902-4151 FAX 360/586-5629

      Cheri Kennedy, Executive Scheduler

Lori Augino, Director of Elections
Elections Division
520 Union Avenue, Southeast
P.O. Box 40229
Olympia, Washington 98504-0229
E-Mail: elections@sos.wa.gov
360/902-4180 FAX 360/664-4619
1-800/448-4881 (Toll Free)

- Candidates on Ballot
- Election Results
- Initiatives
- Motor Voter
- Voters Pamphlet
- Voter Registration
- Voting Accessibility
- Certification and Training

Tsering Cornell, Director of Corporations
Corporations Division
801 Capitol Way South
P.O. Box 40234
Olympia, Washington 98504-0234
E-Mail: corps@sos.wa.gov
360/725-0377

- Corporate Registration
- Charities Registration

WASHINGTON PUBLIC DISCLOSURE COMMISSION

Evelyn Fielding Lopez, Executive Director
Public Disclosure Commission
711 Capitol Way, Room 206
P.O. Box 40908
Olympia, Washington 98504-0908
URL http://www.pdc.wa.gov
E-Mail: pdc@pdc.wa.gov
360/753-1111 FAX 360/753-1112
1-877/601-2828 (Toll Free)

      Lori Anderson, Communications and Training Officer

- Federal Campaign Finance Reports
  (Online via FEC.gov)
- Federal Personal Financial Reports
- State Campaign Finance Reports (Online)
- State Personal Financial Reports
- State Lobby Reports (Online)
- State Initiative/Referendum Spending Reports
  (Online)
- Political Advertising/Sponsor Identification
- Electronic Filings

WASHINGTON STATE EXECUTIVE ETHICS BOARD

Kate Reynolds, Executive Director
Washington State Executive Ethics Board
2425 Bristol Court SW
P.O. Box 40149
Olympia, Washington 98504-0149
URL http://www.ethics.wa.gov
E-Mail: ethics@atg.wa.gov
360/664-0871 FAX 360/586-3955

- Advisory Opinions and Guidance on Ethics Laws
- Enforcement of Ethics Laws

WASHINGTON STATE LEGISLATIVE ETHICS BOARD

Mike O'Connell, Counsel
Legislative Ethics Board
P.O. Box 40600
Olympia, Washington 98504-0600
URL http://leg.wa.gov/leb
E-Mail: oconnell.mike@leg.wa.gov
360/786-7540 FAX 360/786-1553

    Kenny Pittman, Chair

*
* -Issue Advisory Opinions and Guidance on
*   Legislative Ethics Issues
* -Enforcement of Revised Code of Washington,
*   42.52, the State Ethics Act (Legislative)
*
*
*
*
*

SEATTLE ETHICS AND ELECTIONS COMMISSION

Wayne Barnett, Executive Director
Seattle Ethics and Elections Commission
700 Fifth Avenue, Suite 4010
P.O. Box 94729
Seattle, Washington 98124-4729
URL http://www.seattle.gov/ethics
E-Mail: wayne.barnett@seattle.gov
206/684-8500 FAX 206/684-8590

*
* -City Campaign Finance Reports (Online)
* -Enforcement of Ethics Code and Contribution
*   Limits
* -Investigation of Whistleblower Complaints
* -Ethics, Campaign and Committee Training
* -Advisory Opinions on Ethics and Elections Laws
* -Voter Guides
* -Electronic Filings

LEGISLATIVE REFERENCE

Hunter G. Goodman, Secretary of the Senate
Washington State Senate
P.O. Box 40482
Olympia, Washington 98504-0482
URL http://www1.leg.wa.gov/Senate
E-Mail: hunter.goodman@leg.wa.gov
360/786-7550 FAX 360/786-7520

Barbara Baker, Chief Clerk of the House
Washington State House of Representatives
P.O. Box 40600
Olympia, Washington 98504-0600
URL http://www1.leg.wa.gov/House
E-Mail: baker.barbara@leg.wa.gov
360/786-7750 FAX 360/786-7036

ATTORNEY GENERAL

Robert W. Ferguson (Elected, D)
Attorney General of Washington
1125 Washington Street, S.E.
P.O. Box 40100
Olympia, Washington 98504-0100
URL http://www.atg.wa.gov
E-Mail: publicrecords@atg.wa.gov
360/753-6200 FAX 360/586-8474

*
* -Other Court Actions
*
*
*
*
*
*

WEST VIRGINIA

SECRETARY OF STATE

Natalie Tennant (Elected, D)
Secretary of State
Building 1, Suite 157-K
1900 Kanawha Boulevard East
Charleston, West Virginia 25305-0770
URL http://www.wvsos.com
E-Mail: wvsos@wvsos.com
304/558-6000   FAX 304/558-0900
1-866/767-8683 (Toll Free in State)

Layna Brown, Director of Elections
E-Mail: lbrown@wvsos.com
304/558-6000   FAX 304/558-8386

Penney Barker, Director
Business/Licensing Division
Building 1, Suite 157-K
1900 Kanawha Boulevard East
Charleston, West Virginia 25305
E-Mail: pbarker@wvsos.com
304/558-8000   FAX 304/558-8381

* -Candidates on Ballot
* -Election Results
* -Federal Campaign Finance Reports
*   (Online via FEC.gov)
* -HAVA Compliance
* -State Campaign Finance Reports (Online)
* -Centralized Voter Registration
* -Fraud Investigations System
* -Voting Accessibility

* -Corporate Registration
* -Licensing
* -Notary Public
* -Authentication of Documents
* -Charity Registration
* -UCC

WEST VIRGINIA ETHICS COMMISSION

Rebecca L. Stepto, Executive Director
West Virginia Ethics Commission
210 Brooks Street, Suite 300
Charleston, West Virginia 25301
URL http://www.ethics.wv.gov
E-Mail: rebecca.l.stepto@wv.gov
304/558-0664   FAX 304/558-2169
1-866/588-0664 (Toll Free in State)

* -Public Servants at City, County and State
*   Personal Financial Reports
* -Lobbyist Registration and Activity Reports

LEGISLATIVE REFERENCE

Drew Ross, Director
Legislative Reference Library
State Capitol, Room MB-27, Building 1
Charleston, West Virginia 25305-0591
URL http://www.legis.state.wv.us
304/347-4836   FAX 304/347-4901

   Mandi Cardosi, Public Information Officer
   Chris Marshall, Public Information Officer
   DeAnnia Spelock, Resources Manager
   John Tice, Graphic Designer and Art Director
   Perry Bennett, Legislative Photographer
   Martin Valent, Photographer
   Dennis Loudermilk, Web Engineer
   Steve Marsden, Web Developer

* -West Virginia Code
* -Senate and House Journals
* -The Acts of the Legislature
* -Online Access to Current Legislative Session
* -Bill Tracking and Text
* -West Virginia Blue Books

ATTORNEY GENERAL

Patrick Morrisey (Elected, R)
Attorney General of West Virginia
Building 1, Room 26-E
1900 Kanawha Boulevard East
Charleston, West Virginia 25305-0220
URL http://www.ago.wv.gov/
304/558-2021   FAX 304/558-0140

*
*   -Other Court Actions
*   -Consumer Protection
*   -Civil Rights
*
*
*
*

WISCONSIN

SECRETARY OF STATE

Douglas La Follette (Elected, D)
Secretary of State
B 41 West, State Capitol
Madison, Wisconsin 53702
URL http://www.sos.state.wi.us
E-Mail: statesec@sos.state.wi.us
608/266-8888   FAX 608/266-3159
    Mailing Address:
    P.O. Box 7848
    Madison, Wisconsin 53707-7848

WISCONSIN GOVERNMENT ACCOUNTABILITY BOARD

Kevin J. Kennedy, Director and General Counsel
Wisconsin Government Accountability Board*
212 East Washington Avenue, 3rd Floor
Madison, Wisconsin 53703
URL http://gab.wi.gov
E-Mail: gab@wi.gov
608/266-8005   FAX 608/267-0500
    Mailing Address:
    P.O. Box 7984
    Madison, Wisconsin 53707-7984

    Nathan Judnic, Staff Counsel, 608/267-0953
    Reid Magney, Public Information Officer, 608/267-7887

Michael Haas, Administrator
Elections Division
608/266-0136

Jonathan Becker, Administrator
Ethics Division
608/267-0647

  *Note: On June 30, 2016, the Government Accountability Board
  will be replaced by two separate Commissions. The Ethics
  Commission will oversee campaign finance laws, lobbying and
  ethics. The Elections Commission will oversee the administration
  of elections.

- Candidates on Ballot
- Election Results
- Voting Accessibility
- Voter Registration
- Federal Campaign Finance Reports
    (Online via FEC.gov)
- Federal Personal Financial Reports
- State Campaign Finance Reports
    (Online via https://cfis.wi.gov)
- State Personal Financial Reports
    (Elected and Appointed Officials)
- State Lobby Reports
    (Online via https://lobbying.wi.gov)
- Electronic Filings

DEPARTMENT OF FINANCIAL INSTITUTIONS

Lon E. Roberts, Secretary
Department of Financial Institutions
201 West Washington Avenue, Suite 500
Madison, Wisconsin 53703
URL http://www.wdfi.org/
608/264-7800   FAX 608/261-4334

    Division of Corporate and Consumer Services
    P.O. Box 7846
    Madison, Wisconsin 53707-7846
    608/261-7577 FAX 608/267-6813

- Corporate Registration

WISCONSIN (Continued)

STATE TREASURER

Matt Adamczyk (Elected, R)
State Treasurer
B 41 West, State Capitol
Madison, Wisconsin 53701
URL http://www.statetreasury.wisconsin.gov
E-Mail: treasury@ost.state.wi.us
608/266-1714   FAX 608/261-6799
   Mailing Address:
   P.O. Box 2114
   Madison, Wisconsin 53701

   Scott Feldt, Deputy Treasurer
   608/266-7982

-Local Government Investment Pool

LEGISLATIVE REFERENCE BUREAU

Richard Champagne, Chief
Legislative Reference Bureau
One East Main Street, Suite 200
Madison, Wisconsin 53703
URL http://legis.wisconsin.gov/lrb
E-Mail: LRB.Reference@legis.wisconsin.gov
608/266-0341   FAX 608/266-5648
   Mailing Address:
   P.O. Box 2037
   Madison, Wisconsin 53701-2037

-Historical Information on Voting Statistics
   and Legislation
-Election Statistics

ATTORNEY GENERAL

Brad D. Schimel (Elected, R)
Attorney General of Wisconsin
114 East State Capitol
P.O. Box 7857
Madison, Wisconsin 53707-7857
URL http://www.doj.state.wi.us
608/266-1221   FAX 608/267-2779
TTY 800/947-3529

-Other Court Actions

WYOMING

SECRETARY OF STATE

Ed Murray (Elected, R)
Secretary of State
2020 Carey Avenue, Suite 600
Cheyenne, Wyoming 82002-0020
URL http://soswy.state.wy.us
E-Mail: secofstate@wyo.gov
307/777-7378   FAX 307/777-6217

      Karen Wheeler, Deputy Secretary of State

Kai Schon, Election Director
E-Mail: elections@wyo.gov
307/777-5860   FAX 307/777-7640

Jeri Melsness, Director
Business Division
307/777-5407   FAX 307/777-5339

*
* -Candidates on Ballot
* -Election Results
* -Ethics Disclosure
* -Federal Campaign Finance Reports
* (Online via FEC.gov)
* -State Campaign Finance Reports
* -State Initiative/Referendum Spending Reports
* -State Elected Official Financial Disclosure Reports
* -State Lobby Registration
* -Lobbyist Disclosure
* -Voting Accessibility
*
*
*
*
* -Corporate Registration
* -UCC

LEGISLATIVE REFERENCE

Dave Gruver, Director
Legislative Service Office
213 State Capitol
Cheyenne, Wyoming 82002
URL http://legisweb.state.wy.us/LSOWeb/LegislativeServiceOffice.aspx
307/777-7881   FAX 307/777-5466

ATTORNEY GENERAL

Peter K. Michael (Appointed)
Attorney General of Wyoming
2320 Capitol Avenue
Cheyenne, Wyoming 82002
URL http://ag.wyo.gov
307/777-7841   FAX 307/777-6869

* -Other Court Actions

LEGISLATIVE COMMITTEES DEALING WITH ELECTIONS

FEDERAL

Committee on Rules and Administration
U.S. Senate
305 Senate Russell Office Building
Washington, D.C. 20510-6325
URL http://rules.senate.gov/public
202/224-6352 FAX 202/224-1912

Committee on House Administration
U.S. House of Representatives
1309 Longworth House Office Building
Washington, D.C. 20515-6157
URL http://cha.house.gov
202/225-8281 FAX 202/225-9957

ALABAMA

Senate Constitution, Campaign Finance, Ethics and
Elections Committee
State House, Room 731
Montgomery, AL 36130
334/242-7826

House Constitution, Campaigns and Elections Committee
State House, Room 206
Montgomery, AL 36130
334/242-7863

ALASKA

Senate State Affairs Committee
State Capitol, Room 205
Juneau, AK 99801-1182
907/465-6600

House State Affairs Committee
State Capitol
Juneau, AK 99801-1182
907/465-3725

ARIZONA

Senate Judiciary Committee
Capitol Complex, 1700 West Washington
Phoenix, AZ 85007-2890
602/542-4900

House Elections Committee
Capitol Complex, 1700 West Washington
Phoenix, AZ 85007-2890
602/542-4221

ARKANSAS

Senate State Agencies and Governmental Affairs
Committee
320 State Capitol Building
Little Rock, AR 72201
501/682-6107

House State Agencies and Governmental Affairs
Committee
350 State Capitol Building
Little Rock, AR 72201
501/682-7771 or 501/682-6211

CALIFORNIA

Senate Elections and Constitutional Amendments
Committee
State Capitol, Room 3191
Sacramento, CA 95814
916/651-4120

Assembly Elections and Redistricting Committee
1020 N Street, Room 365
Sacramento, CA 95814
916/319-2094

COLORADO

Senate State, Veterans and Military Affairs Committee
State Capitol
200 East Colfax Avenue
Denver, CO 80203-1784
303/866-2316

House State, Veterans and Military Affairs Committee
State Capitol
200 East Colfax Avenue
Denver, CO 80203-1784
303/866-2904

CONNECTICUT

Joint Government Administration and Elections Committee
Legislative Office Building, Room 2200
300 Capitol Avenue
Hartford, CT 06106-1591
860/240-0480

DELAWARE

Senate Administrative Services/Elections Committee
Legislative Hall, P.O. Box 1401
Dover, DE 19903
302/744-4286

House Administration Committee
Legislative Hall, P.O. Box 1401
Dover, DE 19903
302/744-4087

FLORIDA

Senate Ethics and Elections Committee
420 Knott Building, 404 South Monroe Street
Tallahassee, FL 32399-1100
850/487-5828

LEGISLATIVE COMMITTEES DEALING WITH ELECTIONS

FLORIDA

House State Affairs Committee
402 South Monroe Street
Tallahassee, FL 32399-1300
850/717-5400

GEORGIA

Senate Reapportionment and Redistricting Committee
Coverdell Legislative Office Building, Suite 325-A
Atlanta, GA 30334
404/656-0150

House Legislative & Congressional
Reapportionment Committee
Coverdell Legislative Office Building, Suite 402
Legislative Office Building
Atlanta, GA 30334
404/656-0305

HAWAII

Senate Government Operations Committee
State Capitol, 415 S. Beretania Street, Room 219
Honolulu, HI 96813
808/586-6720

House Judiciary Committee
State Capitol, 415 S. Beretania Street, Room 302
Honolulu, HI 96813
808/586-6400

IDAHO

Senate State Affairs Committee
Statehouse, Room WW55
Boise, ID 83720-0081
208/332-1326

House State Affairs Committee
Statehouse, Room EW40
Boise, ID 83720-0038
208/332-1145

ILLINOIS

Senate Local Government Committee
State Capitol
Springfield, IL 62706
217/782-5715

House Rules Committee
State Capitol
Springfield, IL 62706
217/782-8223

INDIANA

Senate Elections Committee
State House, 200 West Washington Street
Indianapolis, IN 46204
317/232-9400

House Elections and Apportionment Committee
State House, 200 West Washington Street
Indianapolis, IN 46204-2786
317/232-9600

IOWA

Senate State Government Committee
State Capitol, Senate Chamber State of Iowa
Des Moines, IA 50319
515/281-3371

House State Government Committee
State Capitol
Des Moines, IA 50319
515/281-3221

KANSAS

Senate Ethics and Elections Committee
Statehouse
Topeka, KS 66612-1504
785/296-2456

House Elections Committee
Statehouse, Room 281-N
Topeka, KS 66612-1504
785/296-7633

KENTUCKY

Senate State and Local Government Committee
State Capitol
Frankfort, KY 40601
502/564-5320

House Elections, Constitutional Amendments and
    Intergovernmental Affairs Committee
State Capitol
Frankfort, KY 40601
502/564-8100

LOUISIANA

Senate and Governmental Affairs Committee
State Capitol, P.O. Box 94183
Baton Rouge, LA 70804
225/342-2040

LEGISLATIVE COMMITTEES DEALING WITH ELECTIONS

House and Governmental Affairs Committee
State Capitol, P.O. Box 94062
Baton Rouge, LA 70804
225/342-6945

MAINE

Senate Rules Committee
3 State House Station
Augusta, ME 04333-0003
207/287-3910

House Elections Committee
2 State House Station
Augusta, ME 04333-0002
207/287-1400

MARYLAND

Senate Rules Committee
State House
Annapolis, MD 21401
410/841-3910

House Ways and Means Committee
131 House Office Building
Annapolis, MD 21401-1912
410/841-3777

MASSACHUSETTS

Senate Committee on Redistricting
State House, Room 413-F
Boston, MA 02133
617/722-1455

House Rules Committee
State House, Room 312-B
Boston, MA 01233
617/722-2000

MICHIGAN

Senate Elections and Government Reform Committee
123 West Allegan Street
Lansing, MI 48933
517/373-2400

House Local Government Committee
P.O. Box 30014
Lansing, MI 48909-7514
517/373-0135

MINNESOTA

Senate State and Local Government Committee
75 Rev. Dr. Martin Luther King Jr., Boulevard, Room 328
St. Paul, MN 55155
651/296-1113

House Government Operations and Elections Policy
  Committee
100 Rev. Dr. Martin Luther King Jr., Boulevard
St. Paul, MN 55155
651/296-2146

MISSISSIPPI

Senate Elections Committee
New Capitol, P.O. Box 1018
Jackson, MS 39215-1018
601/359-3770

House Apportionment and Elections Committee
New Capitol, P.O. Box 1018
Jackson, MS 39215-1018
601/359-3360

MISSOURI

Financial, Governmental Organizations and Elections
  Committee
State Capitol
Jefferson City, MO 65101
573/751-3824

House Elections Committee
State Capitol
Jefferson City, MO 65101
573/751-3829

MONTANA

Senate State Administration Committee
Capitol Station
Helena, MT 59620-1706
406/444-4800

House State Administration Committee
1301 East 5th Avenue
Helena, MT 59601
406/444-4800

NEBRASKA

Government, Military and Veterans Affairs Committee
State Capitol
Lincoln, NE 68509
402/471-2271

NEVADA

Senate Legislative Operations & Elections Committee
Legislative Building, Room 2144
Carson City, NV 89701-4747
775/684-1465

Assembly Legislative Operations and Elections Committee
Legislative Building, Room 3142
Carson City, NV 89701-4747
775/684-8555

LEGISLATIVE COMMITTEES DEALING WITH ELECTIONS

NEW HAMPSHIRE

Senate Public and Municipal Affairs
Legislative Office Building
107 North Main Street
Concord, NH 03301-4951
603/271-2111

House Election Law Committee
Legislative Office Building, Room 308
Concord, NH 03301
603/271-3319

NEW JERSEY

Senate Community & Urban Affairs Committee
State House Annex, P.O. Box 068
Trenton, NJ 08625-0068
609/847-3915

Senate State Government, Wagering, Tourism
and Historic Preservation Committee
State House Annex, P.O. Box 068
Trenton, NJ 08625-0068
609/847-3915

Assembly State and Local Government Committee
State House Annex, P.O. Box 068
Trenton, NJ 08625-0068
609/847-3905

NEW MEXICO

Senate Rules Committee
State Capitol, Room 321
Santa Fe, NM 87501
505/986-4714

House Government, Elections and Indian Affairs
    Committee
State Capitol
Santa Fe, NM 87503
505/986-4751

NEW YORK

Senate Elections Committee
Legislative Office Building
Albany, NY 12248
518/455-2800

Assembly Election Law Committee
Legislative Office Building, Room 715
Albany, NY 12248
518/455-4218

NORTH CAROLINA

Senate State and Local Government Committee
State Legislative Building
Raleigh, NC 27601-2808
919/733-7928

Senate Redistricting Committee
State Legislative Building
Raleigh, NC 27601-2808
919/733-7928

House Elections Committee
Legislative Office Building, Room 1425
Raleigh, NC 27601-1906
919/715-3015

NORTH DAKOTA

Senate Political Subdivisions Committee
State Capitol, 600 East Boulevard
Bismarck, ND 58505-0360
701/328-2916

Senate Government & Veterans Affairs Committee
State Capitol, 600 East Boulevard
Bismarck, ND 58505
701/328-2916

House Political Subdivisions Committee
State Capitol
Bismarck, ND 58505
701/328-2916

House Government & Veterans Affairs Committee
State Capitol
Bismarck, ND 58505
701/328-2916

OHIO

Senate State and Local Government Committee
Senate Building, Room 038
Columbus, OH 43215
614/466-4900

House State Government Committee
77 South High Street
Columbus, OH 43266-0603
614/466-3357

OKLAHOMA

Senate General Government Committee
State Capitol
Oklahoma City, OK 73105
405/524-0126

House Elections and Ethics Committee
State Capitol
Oklahoma City, OK 73105
405/521-2711

OREGON

Senate Rules Committee
State Capitol
Salem, OR 97310
503/986-1851

LEGISLATIVE COMMITTEES DEALING WITH ELECTIONS

OREGON

House Rules, Redistricting and Public Affairs Committee
State Capitol, 900 Court Street NE
Salem, OR 97310
503/986-1000

PENNSYLVANIA

Senate State Government Committee
Capitol Building
Harrisburg, PA 17120-3020
717/787-5920

House State Government Committee
Capitol Building, Box 202220
Harrisburg, PA 17120-2020
717/787-2372

RHODE ISLAND

Senate Rules Committee
State House
Providence, RI 02903
401/222-6655

House Municipal Government Committee
State House
Providence, RI 02903
401/222-2466

House Rules Committee
State House
Providence, RI 02903
401/222-2466

SOUTH CAROLINA

Senate Judiciary Committee
Gressette Building, Room 101
P.O. Box 142
Columbia, SC 29202
803/212-6610

House Judiciary Committee
Blatt Building, Room 512
P.O. Box 11867
Columbia, SC 29211
803/734-3120

SOUTH DAKOTA

Senate State Affairs Committee
500 East Capitol Avenue
Pierre, SD 57501-5070
605/773-3821

House State Affairs Committee
500 East Capitol Avenue
Pierre, SD 57501-5070
605/773-3851

TENNESSEE

Senate State and Local Government Committee
6 Legislative Plaza
Nashville, TN 37243
615/741-7891

House State Government Committee
209 War Memorial Building
Nashville, TN 37243
615/741-2901

TEXAS

Senate State Affairs Committee
State Capitol, Room 380
P.O. Box 12068
Austin, TX 78711
512/463-0100

House Committee on Elections
State Capitol
P.O. Box 2910
Austin, TX 78768-2910
512/463-5896

House Redistricting Committee
State Capitol
P.O. Box 2910
Austin, TX 78768-2910
512/463-5896

UTAH

Senate Government Operations and Political Subdivisions
Committee
350 North State Street, Suite 320
Salt Lake City, UT 84114
801/538-1035

House Government Operations Committee
350 North State Street, Suite 350
Salt Lake City, UT 84114
801/538-1029

VERMONT

Senate Government Operations Committee
State House, 115 State Street, Room 4
Montpelier, VT 05633-5301
802/223-2228

House Government Operations Committee
State House, 115 State Street, Room 49
Montpelier, VT 05633-5301
802/828-2247

VIRGINIA

Senate Privileges and Elections Committee
General Assembly Building
910 Capitol Street, P. O. Box 396
Richmond, VA 23218
804/698-7410

LEGISLATIVE COMMITTEES DEALING WITH ELECTIONS

VIRGINIA

House Privileges and Elections Committee
General Assembly Building
910 Capitol Street, P. O. Box 406
Richmond, VA 23218
804/698-1500

WASHINGTON

Senate Government Operations and State Security
    Committee
201 John A. Cherberg Building
P.O. Box 40466
Olympia, WA 98504-0466
360/786-7400

House State Government Committee
P.O. Box 40600
Olympia, WA 98504-0600
360/786-7573

WEST VIRGINIA

Senate Government Organization Committee
State Capitol
Charleston, WV 25305
304/357-7800

House Government Organization Committee
State Capitol
Charleston, WV 25305
304/340-3200

House Political Subdivisions Committee
State Capitol
Charleston, WV 25305
304/340-3200

WISCONSIN

Senate Elections and Local Government Committee
16W State Capitol, P.O. Box 7882
Madison, WI 53707-7882
608/266-2517

Assembly Campaigns and Elections Committee
115W State Capitol, P.O. Box 8952
Madison, WI 53708
608/266-1501

WYOMING

Senate Corporations, Elections and Political Subdivisions
Committee
State Capitol
Cheyenne, WY 82002
307/777-7711

House Corporations, Elections and Political Subdivisions
Committee
State Capitol
Cheyenne, WY 82002
307/777-7852

DISTRICT OF COLUMBIA

Committee on the Judiciary
1350 Pennsylvania Avenue, NW
Washington, D.C. 20004
202/727-8275

AMERICAN SAMOA

Senate Legal Affairs Committee
P.O. Box 485
Pago Pago, AS 96799
684/633-5866

House Local Government/TAOA/ Election Committee
P.O. Box 485
Pago Pago, AS 96799
684/633-5763

GUAM

Committee on Rules, Federal Affairs and Election Reform
Guam Legislature
155 Hesler Place
Hagatna, Guam 96910
671/472-3499

PUERTO RICO

Senate Government, Government Efficiency and Economic
    Innovation Committee
Puerto Rico Senate, The Capitol
P.O. Box 9023431
San Juan, Puerto Rico 00902-3431
787/724-2030

House Government Committee
Puerto Rico House of Representatives, The Capitol
P.O. Box 9022228
San Juan, Puerto Rico 00902-2228
787/721-6040

U.S. VIRGIN ISLANDS

Government Rules and Judiciary Committee
Capitol Building
P.O. Box 1690
Charlotte Amalie
St. Thomas, USVI 00804
340/774-0880

LEGISLATIVE COMMITTEES DEALING WITH ETHICS

FEDERAL

Select Committee on Ethics
U.S. Senate
220 Senate Hart Office Building
Washington, D.C. 20510-6425
URL http://ethics.senate.gov/public
202/224-2981 FAX 202/224-7416

Committee on Ethics
U.S. House of Representatives
1015 Longworth House Office Building
Washington, D.C. 20515
URL http://ethics.house.gov
202/225-7103 FAX 202/225-7392

ALABAMA

Senate Rules Committee
State House, Room 729
Montgomery, AL 36130
334/242-7853

House Rules Committee
State House, Room 519-C
Montgomery, AL 36130
334/242-7673

ALASKA

Select Committee on Legislative Ethics
P.O. Box 101468
Anchorage, AK 99510-1468
907/269-0150

ARIZONA

Senate Rules Committee
Capitol Complex, 1700 West Washington
Phoenix, AZ 85007-2890
602/926-4900

House Rules Committee
Capitol Complex, 1700 West Washington
Phoenix, AZ 85007-2890
602/926-4221

ARKANSAS

Senate State Agencies and Governmental Affairs
Committee
State Capitol
Little Rock, AR 72201
501/682-6107

House State Agencies and Governmental Affairs
Committee
State Capitol
Little Rock, AR 72201
501/682-7771 or 501/682-6211

CALIFORNIA

Senate Committee on Legislative Ethics
1020 N Street, Suite 238
Sacramento, CA 95814
916/651-1507

Assembly Rules Committee
State Capitol, Room 3016
Sacramento, CA 95814
916/319-2856

COLORADO

Senate Judiciary Committee
State Capitol
200 East Colfax
Denver, CO 80203
303/866-2316

House Judiciary Committee
State Capitol
200 East Colfax
Denver, CO 80203
303/866-2904

CONNECTICUT

Joint Government Administration and Elections Committee
Legislative Office Building, Room 2200
300 Capitol Avenue
Hartford, CT 06106-1591
860/240-0480

DELAWARE

Senate Ethics Committee
Legislative Hall, P.O. Box 1401
Dover, DE 19903
302/744-4286

House Ethics Committee
Legislative Hall, P.O. Box 1401
Dover, DE 19903
302/744-4087

FLORIDA

Senate Ethics and Elections Committee
420 Knott Building, 404 South Monroe Street
Tallahassee, FL 32399-1100
850/487-5828

House Rules and Calendar Committee
402 South Monroe Street
Tallahassee, FL 32399-1300
850/717-5400

GEORGIA

Senate Ethics Committee
State Capitol, Room 321
Atlanta, GA 30334
404/656-0089

House Ethics Committee
613 Legislative Office Building
Atlanta, GA 30334
404/656-0305

LEGISLATIVE COMMITTEES DEALING WITH ETHICS

HAWAII

Senate Judiciary and LaborCommittee
State Capitol, 415 S. Beretania Street
Honolulu, HI 96813
808/586-6720

House Judiciary Committee
State Capitol, 415 S. Beretania Street, Room 325
Honolulu, HI 96813
808/586-6400

IDAHO

Senate Judiciary and Rules Committee
Statehouse, Room WW54
Boise, ID 83720-0081
208/332-1317

House Judiciary, Rules and Administration Committee
Statehouse, Room EW42
Boise, ID 83720-0038
208/332-1127

ILLINOIS

Senate Executive Appointments Committee
121 B Capitol Building
Springfield, IL 62706
217/782-5715

House Executive Committee
State Capitol
Springfield, IL 62706
217/782-8223

INDIANA

Senate Ethics Committee
200 West Washington Street
Indianapolis, IN 46204
317/232-9400

House Statutory Committee On Ethics
200 West Washington Street
Indianapolis, IN 46204
317/232-9600

IOWA

Senate Ethics Committee
State Capitol, Senate Chamber State of Iowa
1015 East Grand
Des Moines, IA 50319
515/281-3371

House Ethics Committee
State Capitol
Des Moines, IA 50319
515/281-3221

KANSAS

Senate Ethics and Elections Committee
Statehouse
Topeka, KS 66612-1504
785/296-2456

House Federal and State Affairs Committee
Statehouse
Topeka, KS 66612-1504
785/296-7633

KENTUCKY

Senate State and Local Government Committee
State Capitol
Frankfort, KY 40601
502/564-5320

House State Government Committee
State Capitol
Frankfort, KY 40601
502/564-8100

LOUISIANA

Senate and Governmental Affairs Committee
State Capitol, P.O. Box 94183
Baton Rouge, LA 70804
225/342-2040

House and Governmental Affairs Committee
State Capitol, P.O. Box 94062
Baton Rouge, LA 70804
225/342-6945

MAINE

Senate Conduct and Ethics Committee
3 State House Station
Augusta, ME 04333-0003
207/287-1540

House Ethics Committee
2 State House Station
Augusta, ME 04333-0002
207/287-1400

MARYLAND

Joint Committee on Legislative Ethics
90 State Circle, Room 200
Annapolis, MD 21401-1991
410/946-5200

MASSACHUSETTS

Senate Committee on Ethics and Rules
State House, Room 333
Boston, MA 02133
617/722-1455

House Standing Committee on Ethics
State House, Room 504
Boston, MA 02133
617/722-2000

LEGISLATIVE COMMITTEES DEALING WITH ETHICS

MICHIGAN

Senate Judiciary Committee
123 West Allegan Street
Lansing, MI 48933
517/373-2400

House Oversight and Ethics Committee
P.O. Box 30014
Lansing, MI 48909-7514
517/373-0135

MINNESOTA

Senate Rules & Administration Committee
State Capitol, Room 208
St. Paul, MN 55155
651/296-2577

House Ethics Committee
State Office Building
St. Paul, MN 55155
651/296-2146

MISSISSIPPI

Senate Ethics Committee
New Capitol, P.O. Box 1018
Jackson, MS 39215-1018
601/359-3770

House Ethics Committee
New Capitol, P.O. Box 1018
Jackson, MS 39215-1018
601/359-3360

MISSOURI

Senate Rules, Joint Rules, Resolutions and Ethics
    Committee
State Capitol
Jefferson City, MO 65101
573/751-3824

House Ethics Committee
State Capitol
Jefferson City, MO 65101
573/751-3829

MONTANA

Senate Ethics Committee
Capitol Station
Helena, MT 59620-0500
406/444-4800

House Ethics Committee
1301 East 5th Avenue
Helena, MT 59601
406/444-4800

NEBRASKA

Government, Military and Veterans Affairs Committee
State Capitol
Lincoln, NE 68509
402/471-2271

NEVADA

Senate Legislative Operations & Elections Committee
Legislative Building, Room 2144
Carson City, NV 89701-4747
775/684-1465

Assembly Legislative Operations and Elections Committee
Legislative Building, Room 3142
Carson City, NV 89701-4747
775/684-8555

NEW HAMPSHIRE

Senate Rules, Enrolled Bills and Internal Affairs
    Committee
State House, Room 200
Concord, NH 03301
603/271-2111

House Legislative Administration Committee
Legislative Office Building, Room 104
Concord, NH 03301
603/271-3317

NEW JERSEY

Joint Legislative Committee on Ethical Standards
State House Annex, P.O. Box 068
Trenton, NJ 08625-0068
609/292-4625

NEW MEXICO

Senate Judiciary Committee
State Capitol, Room 321
Santa Fe, NM 87503
505/986-4714

House Judiciary Committee
State Capitol, Room 309
Santa Fe, NM 87503
505/986-4751

NEW YORK

Senate Ethics Committee
Legislative Office Building
Albany, NY 12248
518/455-2800

Assembly Ethics and Guidance Committee
Legislative Office Building, Room 557
Albany, NY 12248
518/455-4218

LEGISLATIVE COMMITTEES DEALING WITH ETHICS

NORTH CAROLINA

Senate Rules and Operation of the Senate Committee
State Legislative Building
Raleigh, NC 27601
919/733-7928

House Ethics Committee
Legislative Office Building
Raleigh, NC 27601
919/733-7928

NORTH DAKOTA

Senate Judiciary Committee
State Capitol
600 East Boulevard
Bismarck, ND 58505-0360
701/328-2916

House Judiciary Committee
State Capitol
Bismarck, ND 58505
701/328-2916

OHIO

Joint Legislative Ethics Committee
50 West Broad Street, Suite 1308
Columbus, OH 43215-5908
614/728-5100

Senate Oversight and Reform Committee
Senate Building
Columbus, OH 43215
614/466-4900

House Government Accountability and Oversight
   Committee
77 South High Street
Columbus, OH 43266-0603
614/466-3357

OKLAHOMA

Senate Rules Committee
State Capitol
Oklahoma City, OK 73105
405/524-0126

House Rules Committee
State Capitol
Oklahoma City, OK 73105
405/521-2711

House Elections and Ethics Committee
State Capitol
Oklahoma City, OK 73105
405/521-2711

House Government Accountability and Oversight
   Committee
State Capitol
Oklahoma City, OK 73105
405/521-2711

OREGON

Senate Rules Committee
State Capitol
Salem, OR 97310
503/986-1851

House Conduct Committee
State Capitol
900 Court Street NE
Salem, OR 97310
503/986-1000

PENNSYLVANIA

Senate Judiciary Committee
Capitol Building
Harrisburg, PA 17120-3012
717/787-5920

House Ethics Committee
Capitol Building, House Box 202020
Harrisburg, PA 17120-2020
717/787-2372

RHODE ISLAND

Senate Government Oversight Committee
State House
Providence, RI 02903
401/276-6655

House Oversight Committee
State House
Providence, RI 02903
401/222-2466

SOUTH CAROLINA

Senate Ethics Committee
Gressette Building, Room 205
P.O. Box 142
Columbia, SC 29202
803/212-6410

House Ethics Committee
Blatt Building, Room 519
P.O. Box 11867
Columbia, SC 29211
803/734-3114

SOUTH DAKOTA

Senate State Affairs
500 East Capitol Avenue
Pierre, SD 57501-5070
605/773-3821

Senate Government Operations and Audit Committee
500 East Capitol Avenue
Pierre, SD 57501-5070
605/773-3821

LEGISLATIVE COMMITTEES DEALING WITH ETHICS

House State Affairs Committee
500 East Capitol Avenue
Pierre, SD 57501-5070
605/773-3851

House Government Operations and Audit Committee
500 East Capitol Avenue
Pierre, SD 57501-5070
605/773-3851

TENNESSEE

Senate Government Operations Committee
307 War Memorial Building
Nashville, TN 37243
615/741-3642

House Government Operations Committee
215 War Memorial Building
Nashville, TN 37243
615/741-2901

TEXAS

State Affairs Committee
Sam Houston Building, Room 380
P.O. Box 12068
Austin, TX 78711
512/463-0100

House Committee on State Affairs
State Capitol
P.O. Box 2910
Austin, TX 78768-2910
512/463-5896

House General Investigating and Ethics Committee
State Capitol
P.O. Box 2910
Austin, TX 78768-2910
512/463-5896

House Government Transparency and Operations
Committee
State Capitol
P.O. Box 2910
Austin, TX 78768-2910
512/463-5896

UTAH

Senate Ethics Committee
350 North State Street, Suite 320
Salt Lake City, UT 84114
801/538-1035

House Ethics Committee
350 North State Street, Suite 350
Salt Lake City, UT 84114
801/538-1029

VERMONT

Senate Judiciary Committee
115 State Street
Montpelier, VT 05633-5301
802/828-2241

Senate Rules Committee
115 State Street
Montpelier, VT 05633-5301
802/828-2241

House Rules Committee
115 State Street
Montpelier, VT 05633-5301
802/828-2247

VIRGINIA

Senate Rules Committee
General Assembly Building
910 Capitol Street, P.O. Box 396
Richmond, VA 23218
804/698-7410

House Rules Committee
General Assembly Building
910 Capitol Street, P.O. 406
Richmond, VA 23218
804/698-1500

WASHINGTON

Senate Rules Committee
201 John A. Cherberg Building, P.O. Box 40466
Olympia, WA 98504-0466
360/786-7400

House Rules Committee
435 John L. O'Brien Building
P.O. Box 40600
Olympia, WA 98504-0600
360/786-7573

WEST VIRGINIA

Senate Rules Committee
State Capitol
Charleston, WV 25305
304/357-7800

House Rules Committee
State Capitol
Charleston, WV 25305
304/340-3200

WISCONSIN

Senate Government Organization Committee
16W. State Capitol, P.O. Box 7882
Madison, WI 53707-7882
608/266-2517

Senate Labor and Government Reform Committee
16W. State Capitol, P.O. Box 7882
Madison, WI 53707-7882
608/266-2517

LEGISLATIVE COMMITTEES DEALING WITH ETHICS

WISCONSIN

Assembly Constitution and Ethics Committee
16W. State Capitol, P.O. Box 8953
Madison, WI 53708-8953
608/266-1501

WYOMING

Senate Rules and Procedure Committee
State Capitol
Cheyenne, WY 82002
307/777-7711

House Rules and Procedure Committee
State Capitol
Cheyenne, WY 82002
307/777-7852

DISTRICT OF COLUMBIA

Committee on the Judiciary
1350 Pennsylvania Avenue, NW
Washington, D.C. 20004
202/727-8275

AMERICAN SAMOA

Senate Rules Committee
P.O. Box 485
Pago Pago, AS 96799
684/633-5866

House Legal Affairs/Judiciary Committee
P.O. Box 485
Pago Pago, AS 96799
684/633-5763

GUAM

Committee on Rules, Federal Affairs and Election Reform
Guam Legislature
155 Hesler Place
Hagatna, Guam 96910
671/472-3499

PUERTO RICO

Senate Ethics Committee
Puerto Rico Senate, The Capitol
P.O. Box 902341
San Juan, PR 00902-3431
787/724-2030

House Ethics Committee
Puerto Rico House of Representatives
P.O. Box 902228
San Juan, Puerto Rico 00902-2228
787/721-6040

U.S. VIRGIN ISLANDS

Senate Rules and Judiciary Committee
Capitol Building
P.O. Box 1690
Charlotte Amalie
St. Thomas, USVI 00804
340/774-0880

OTHER INFORMATION SOURCES

NATIONAL AND INTERNATIONAL ASSOCIATIONS DEALING WITH CAMPAIGN FINANCE AND ELECTIONS

COUNCIL ON GOVERNMENTAL ETHICS LAWS

Diane Gill, CAE
Larry Gill, CPA
Executive Directors
Council on Governmental Ethics Laws
P.O. Box 81237
Athens, Georgia 30608
URL http://www.cogel.org
E-Mail: director@cogel.org
706/548-7758 FAX 706/548-7079

-Liaison for Government Agencies and
    Organizations Concerned with Ethics,
    Elections, Campaign Finance and Lobbying
    Laws

NATIONAL ASSOCIATION OF SECRETARIES OF STATE

Leslie Reynolds, Executive Director
National Association of Secretaries of State
Hall of the States
444 North Capitol Street, N.W., Suite 401
Washington, DC 20001
URL http://www.nass.org
E-Mail: nass@sso.org, reynolds@sso.org
202/624-3525 FAX 202/624-3527

Kay Stimson, Communications and Special Projects Director
Stacy Dodd, Executive Assistant/Meeting Coordinator

NATIONAL ASSOCIATION OF STATE ELECTION DIRECTORS

Tim Mattice, Executive Director
National Association of State Election Directors
c/o The Election Center
21946 Royal Montreal Drive, Suite 100
Katy, Texas 77450
URL http://www.nased.org and *http://www.electioncenter.org/*
E-Mail: services@nased.org and *services@electioncenter.org*
281/396-4314, 281/396-4309 FAX 281/396-4315

NATIONAL CONFERENCE OF STATE LEGISLATURES

William T. Pound, Executive Director
National Conference of State Legislatures
7700 East First Place
Denver, Colorado 80230
URL http://www.ncsl.org
303/364-7700 FAX 303/364-7800

Washington Office:
444 North Capitol Street, N.W., Suite 515
Washington, D.C. 20001
202/624-5400 FAX 202/737-1069

NATIONAL ASSOCIATION OF ATTORNEYS GENERAL

James McPherson, Executive Director
National Association of Attorneys General
2030 M Street, 8th Floor
Washington, D.C. 20036
URL http://www.naag.org
202/326-6000 FAX 202/331-1427

NATIONAL ASSOCIATION OF COUNTIES

Matthew Chase, Executive Director
National Association of Counties
25 Massachusetts Avenue, N.W., Suite 500
Washington, D.C. 20001-2080
URL http://www.naco.org
202/393-6226 FAX 202/393-2630

NATIONAL ASSOCIATION OF COUNTY RECORDERS, ELECTION OFFICIALS AND CLERKS

Suzanne Biegenzahn, Executive Director
National Association of County Recorders, Election Officials and Clerks
2501 Aerial Center Parkway, Suite 103
Morrisville, North Carolina 27560
URL http://www.nacrc.org
E-Mail: info@nacrc.org
919/459-2080 FAX 919/459-2075

INTERNATIONAL ASSOCIATION OF CLERKS, RECORDERS, ELECTION OFFICIALS AND TREASURERS

Brenda Bell, Chief Administrator
International Association Of Clerks, Recorders, Election Officials
    and Treasurers
156 Old Pond Lane
Statesville, North Carolina 28625
URL http://www.iacreot.com
E-Mail: bell42014@gmail.com
1-800/890-7368

INTERNATIONAL FOUNDATION FOR ELECTION SYSTEMS

William "Bill" Sweeney, President/CEO
International Foundation for Election Systems
2011 Crystal Drive, 10th Floor
Arlington, VA 22202
URL http://www.ifes.org
E-Mail: info.communications@ifes.org
202/350-6700 FAX 202/350-6701

INTERNATIONAL INSTITUTE OF MUNICIPAL CLERKS

Chris Shalby, Executive Director
International Institute of Municipal Clerks
8331 Utica Avenue, Suite 200
Rancho Cucamonga, California 91730
URL http://www.iimc.com
E-Mail: Hq@iimc.com
909/944-4162   FAX 909/944-8545
1-800/251-1639 (Toll Free)

*
*
*
*
*
*
*
*
*

ADDITIONAL REFERENCES

The following publications provide additional information on state laws and the specific duties of various offices.

The Book of the States: 2016 edition, published by The Council of State Governments, 2760 Research Park Drive, Lexington, KY 40511, http://csgstore.org/thebookofthestates.aspx, e-mail: sales@csg.org, 1-800/800-1910.

COGEL Blue Book: Campaign Finance Update: A comprehensive look at campaign finance legislation and litigation in the 50 states and the federal government. Copies may be purchased from COGEL, P.O. Box 81237, Athens, GA, 30608, 706/548-7758.

COGEL Blue Book: Ethics Update: Update of events, issues and trends related to organization and administration of ethics boards. Copies may be purchased from COGEL, P.O. Box 81237, Athens, GA, 30608, 706/548-7758.

COGEL Blue Book: Lobbying Update: Summary of current issues and developments in lobby law. Copies may be purchased from COGEL, P.O. Box 81237, Athens, GA, 30608, 706/548-7758.

The Electoral College, January 2011. Published by the U.S. Election Assistance Commission, 1335 East West Highway, Suite 4300, Silver Spring, MD 20910, http://www.eac.gov/voter_resources/the_electoral_college.aspx, 1-866/747-1471 or 301/563-3919.

The Guardian: Quarterly reporting by state agencies on the most recent developments in governmental ethics, campaign finance and lobby law activity. Annual subscriptions are available from COGEL, P.O. Box 81237, Athens, GA, 30608, 706/548-7758.

Public Integrity Journal: Quarterly journal on ethics and leadership for public service. Contact the American Society of Public Administration, http://www.aspanet.org/public/ASPA/Publications/ASPA/Publications/Publications1.aspx, 1730 Rhode Island Avenue, N.W., Suite 500, Washington, DC 20036, e-mail: info@aspanet.org, 202/393-7878.

State Directory I: Elective Officials, 2016 edition, published by The Council of State Governments, 2760 Research Park Drive, Lexington, KY 40511, http://csgstore.org, e-mail: sales@csg.org, 1-800/800-1910.

State Directory II: Legislative Leadership, Committees & Staff, 2016 edition, published by The Council of State Governments, 2760 Research Park Drive, Lexington, KY 40511, http://csgstore.org, e-mail: sales@csg.org, 1-800/800-1910.

State Directory III: Administrative Officials, 2016 edition, published by The Council of State Governments, 2760 Research Park Drive, Lexington, KY 40511, http://csgstore.org, e-mail: sales@csg.org, 1-800/800-1910.

State Legislatures magazine, published by the National Conference of State Legislatures, reports on legislation in the 50 states, best practices, the legislative process and institution, and federal initiatives that affect the states. Annual subscriptions may be purchased from NCSL, Publications Order Desk, 7700 East First Place, Denver, CO 80230, http://comm.ncsl.org/Default.aspx?TabID=251&productId=8, e-mail: books@ncsl.org, 303/364-7812

A Voter's Guide to Federal Elections, August 2014. Available in eleven languages. Published by the U.S. Election Assistance Commission, 1335 East West Highway, Suite 4300, Silver Spring, MD 20910, http://www.eac.gov/voter_resources/a_voters_guide_to_federal_elections.aspx, 1-866/747-1471 or 301/563-3919.

www.ingramcontent.com/pod-product-compliance
Lightning Source LLC
Chambersburg PA
CBHW081148280526
45787CB00008B/3250